Drained

Stories of People
Who Wanted More

Johann Christoph Arnold

Plough Publishing House

© 1999 by Plough Publishing House

Walden, New York
Robertsbridge, England
Elsmore, Australia

Cover photograph © The Stock Market

Vedran Smailovic co-wrote his story (pp. 109–112) with Frances McDonnell.

A catalogue record for this book is available from the British Library.

Library of Congress Cataloging-in-Publication Data

Arnold, Johann Christoph, 1940-
    Drained : stories of people who wanted more / Johann Christoph
Arnold.
       p.   cm.
    ISBN 0-87486-970-6 (softcover)
    1. Christian life--The Bruderhof Foundation authors.   I. Title.
BV4501.2.A735   1999
248.4'8973--dc21   99-18719
                                                  CIP

ISBN 978-0-87486-970-5

To those who refuse to run on empty.

Contents

Acknowledgements

At the heart of this book are real-life stories, and I would like to thank the many people who allowed me to use their personal anecdotes and letters. Your trust has made this book possible.

To the entire Plough team and my editors, Chris Voll and Paul Hansford – my thanks to each of you.

Above all I thank my wife, Verena, for her ever-present encouragement and support.

Prologue: Wanting More

Only when you have made peace
within yourself will you be able
to make peace in the world.

RABBI SIMCHA BUNIM

While working on this book, I came across an advert featuring a picture of a woman curled up in a lawn chair, gazing out over a lake toward a brilliant sunset. The advert reads: 'A dream job. Beautiful kids. The best marriage. And a gnawing feeling of absolute emptiness.' How many millions share her unspoken anxiety?

We work hard, play hard, love hard – and try to isolate ourselves on little islands of sanity in the midst of a raging sea in which stock markets surge and crash, biotech engineers redefine life's boundaries and fashion designers dictate dress code. But somehow the tide keeps rising… And sometimes we're too tired – too drained – even to care. We're tempted to shut our eyes and just pretend it will all go away.

Of course, 'it' never does.

Whether we admit it or not, at a certain level all of us are in continual search for a life we can feel good about living – one where elusive ideals like harmony, joy, justice and peace are everyday realities. In the words of Monty Python, we're looking 'for something completely different'. Each of us has dreamed of a life where sorrow and pain do not exist. At the same time, none of us will deny that violence affects public life everywhere around our globe, from current hot spots to the streets of our own decaying cities. In personal life too, even in the most 'peaceful' suburbs, conflict is often the order of the day – in domestic violence, unhealthy addictions and the destructive tensions that divide businesses, schools and communities.

Violence hides behind the most respectable façades of our supposedly enlightened society. It is there in the turbines of greed, deceit and injustice that drive our greatest financial and cultural institutions. It is there in the infidelity that can erode even the strongest of marriages. It is there in the hypocrisy that deadens our spiritual life and robs even the most devout expressions of religion of so much of their credibility.

Some of us look for fulfilment and peace by modifying our lifestyles: by changing careers, moving from the city to the suburbs (or from the suburbs to the country), cutting back, simplifying, or otherwise trying to improve our quality of life. But all too often, the peace we're seeking continues to elude us. We know all too well that ours is a world in ferment, and that despite constant talk about peace, there is very little. So little, in fact, that when I told a close friend about my plans for this book, he suggested it was not only naïve to write on the topic, but even somewhat perverse.

Against this dismal backdrop, it may indeed seem perverse to write a book on finding peace. Yet the longing for peace and harmony remains unchanged, and it is as ancient as it is universal. Thousands of years ago, the Jewish visionary Isaiah dreamed of a time and place where the lion would dwell peacefully with the lamb. And down through the centuries, no matter how dark the horizon or bloody the battlefield, men and women have found hope in his dream.

For the most part, however, our society has stripped 'peace' of any significant meaning. From greeting cards to bookmarks, from billboards to embroidered tea-towels, our culture is awash with the language of peace. Especially at Christmastime, phrases such as 'peace and good will' appear so widely that they have been reduced to slogans and clichés. On another level, governments and the mass media speak of heavily armed 'peacekeeping' battalions stationed in war-torn regions around the world. In churches, priests and ministers close their services with 'go in peace', and though the words are intended as a blessing, they often seem to be little more than a dismissal until the following Sunday.

Call it what you will, the yearning for peace exists deep in every human being. We all hate stress, headaches, heartaches. We don't like feeling drained. We all want freedom from anxiety and doubt, violence and division. We all want stability and security. Peace.

But though so many of us hanker after peace, we generally want an easy peace – on our own terms. The problem with this is that peace cannot come quickly or easily if it is to have any genuine staying power. It cannot merely mean temporary psychological well-being or equilibrium, a pleasant feeling that is here today and gone tomorrow. True peace is not a commodity to be had or bought. Nor is it a cause that can be taken up and pursued simply with good intentions. Paradoxically, real peace demands struggle. It is found by taking up the fundamental battles of life: life versus death, good versus evil, truth versus falsehood. It is a gift, but it is also the result of the most intense striving.

In our search for peace, perhaps nothing is so vital – or painful – as first coming to terms with the lack of peace in our own lives, with the arid places of our hearts. For some of us this may mean confronting hatred or resentment; for others, deceit, divided loyalties or confusion; for still others, mere emptiness or depression. In the deepest sense it is all violence, and must therefore be faced and overcome.

In the following pages I have tried to resist formulating neat theses or presenting loophole-proof arguments. I have also tried to avoid dwelling on the roots of our feeling of being drained. Though one could write a whole book on that subject, it would be too depressing to wade through. What's more, it might not even help.

Sadhu Sundar Singh, an Indian Christian mystic who lived at the turn of the twentieth century, used an analogy to show how the 'secret and reality of a blissful life' cannot be discovered through intellectual probing:

> A scientist had a bird in his hand. He saw that it had life and, wanting to find out in what part of the bird's body its life lay, he began dissecting the bird. The result was that the very life he was in search of disappeared. Those who try to understand the mysteries of the inner life intellectually will meet with similar failure. The life they are looking for will vanish in the analysis.

Spiritual 'how-to' guides can be found in any bookshop, but in my experience life is never so tidy as they suggest. More often than not, it's a tangled mess. Many of the stories told in this book come from friends of mine, some whom I've known for years, and others only for a short time. Few of them claim to 'have peace' as a permanent state of being. Rather, they attest to the journey that leads towards peace, towards that hard-to-define 'more' we all want. Each of us will be at a different place in our search. My aim in this book, very simply, has been to offer you stepping stones along the way – and enough hope to keep you going.

Life in the Slow Lane

A man is in bondage
to whatever he cannot part with
that is less than himself.

GEORGE MACDONALD

n a 'trends' item, *Time* magazine reported on a
young couple who moved away from their wealthy Ohio
suburb because the woman was sick of living in a neighbourhood where people 'spend all their time working their
backs off so they can fill their big, empty houses with expensive
crap'. She wanted 'serenity, simplicity, some peace of mind'.

At first, life in their new small-town surroundings seemed
perfect, but before long, joblessness pushed the crime rate up,
and trouble with narrow-minded neighbours brought headaches. Determined not to give up, the woman threw herself
into historic real-estate renovation and school board issues.
This didn't seem to bring fulfilment either. Finally the couple
hit on a great plan for achieving the serene lifestyle they so
wanted: they headed off to New England's Nantucket island
to start a bed-and-breakfast...

In the last twenty-five years alone, new inventions and
improvements have utterly transformed the way we live. Com-
puters, phones and other hi-tech labour-saving conveniences

have revolutionized our homes and workplaces. Yet have they brought us the peace and freedom they seemed to promise?

Without realizing it we have become dulled, if not brainwashed, in our eagerness to embrace technology. We have become slaves to a system that presses us to spend money on new gadgets, and we have accepted without question the argument that, by working harder, we will have more time to do more important things. It is a perverse logic. When upgrades on everything from software to cars keep us on the constant run; when we are always struggling to keep up with the Joneses (even against our better judgement), we ought to ask ourselves what we have saved, and whether our lives are any more peaceful.

If anything, the increasing complexity of life today has only robbed us of peace and resulted in a quiet but widespread epidemic of nervousness, insecurity and confusion. Fifty years ago German educator Friedrich Wilhelm Foerster wrote:

> More than ever before, our technical civilization has cushioned life on all sides, yet more than ever, people helplessly succumb to the blows of life. This is very simply because a merely material, technical culture cannot give help in the face of tragedy. The man of today, externalized as he is, has no ideas, no strength, to enable him to master his own restlessness and division…. He has no peace.

Our culture is not only marked by frenzy, but driven by it. We are obsessed (to quote American monk Thomas Merton) with our lack of time and space: with saving time, with conquering space, with making conjectures about the future, and 'worrying about size, volume, quantity, speed, number, price, power and acceleration'.

drained

As the couple who moved to Nantucket found, simplicity cannot be an end in itself. I have no idea whether they ever succeeded in finding the unhampered calm they so much craved. But I have learnt – through my own experiences and those of others – that simplicity can be as elusive as peace of mind. Nature abhors a vacuum, and our attempts to empty our lives of clutter will often achieve nothing more in the long run than clearing space for *new* clutter. If we are disillusioned with a materialistic lifestyle and want to escape its clutches, more will be required of us than a change of pace.

Nonetheless simplicity remains something we must strive for continually when possessions and activities and agendas distract us from the important things of life – family, friends, meaningful relationships and constructive work. These are the things that connect us and draw us together.

Born in the East German city of Dresden to parents dedicated to Communist Party ideals, Stefan grew up fully aware that a world of material bounty lay just beyond his grasp – on the far side of the Berlin Wall. In primary school, students learned the principles of Marxism and listened as teachers expounded on the vision of a classless society. On the playground, however, Stefan and his friends swapped Western gimmicks – Matchbox cars were all the rage – and conjured up their own images of the mysterious place called 'the West'.

> Most of my growing-up years, my parents, my three brothers and I lived in a tower block flat, in a neighbourhood of tower blocks. A lot of people lived like that, and looking back, I'd say it was like living in a bunker, but at that time I never thought like that. I mean, how many people in the world have a roof over their head? We certainly never went hungry. And we had running water, hot and cold. There were no water metres; the bill was the same, regardless of how much you used.

When I was thirteen, I was selected to attend a special sports school, and I left home and began training in judo. The trainers at the school tried to impress on us how important our task was. Everything was geared towards the Olympic Games. We were told that if a member of an Eastern Bloc country were to win a gold medal, it would strike a major blow against imperialism.

It was hard to figure out why they made such a big deal out of everything. As young teenagers, we could never understand why artists like Michael Jackson or Bruce Springsteen couldn't just come over to the East and give concerts.

By the time I reached secondary school age, I was feeling pretty disillusioned. I could see that communism wasn't everything it was chalked up to be – it was just bureaucracy. At the same time, I didn't think capitalism was much of an answer, either; our schooling made us aware of injustices and exploitation going on in Western countries.

I was seventeen when the Berlin Wall came down, in November 1989, and I couldn't have cared less. Sure, there was a certain amount of natural excitement. But it seemed a bit overdone: 'Finally freedom! We can unite with our brothers and sisters in the West.' But it didn't seem to me that people cared very much about their brothers and sisters in the West; they were much more interested in the well-stocked department stores. And people in the West seemed far more intent on gaining access to the East's markets than on befriending its people.

A few days before Christmas I went into former West Berlin, just to check it out. A lot of people had moved into the city, and others went shopping as often as they could, coming back loaded with stuff. But I had a hard time spending any money at all; I only bought a few chocolate bars. As I walked past all those jam-packed shop displays and gazed up at the billboards, I just couldn't imagine living in such an environment.

Both communism and capitalism seemed to fall woefully short of the truth. So I began to dream about other alternatives.

I planned it out in my head, and even drew up my ideas on paper: a place where everyone got along, where poverty didn't exist. Life would be simple and unhurried, and people would have time for each other.

Not long after that, a friend told me about a small, rural community near Cologne, where men and women actually lived and worked together in a money-free environment. I made my first visit and was impressed by their no-frills lifestyle and their commitment to honest, straightforward relationships. A year later I returned to stay. I had found the 'third way' I had been looking for.

Looking back, I know that the lifestyle of my childhood was simple, by Western standards. We didn't choose to live that way; that's just how it was. Today I meet people who make a big deal out of living simply – they won't drink supermarket milk, or they'll only eat whole-wheat bread. There are people who live simply because they can't afford anything better, and there are those who live simply because of a social consciousness, or something.

To me, simplicity for its own sake is pointless. But when it results from a decision to stand against the trend of hand-over-fist accumulation, and to give rather than to get, then simplicity is a fruit of the truth.

2 Noise Pollution

Words are, of course,
the most powerful drug
used by mankind.

RUDYARD KIPLING

One of the biggest drains on our energy and emotion, and one of the greatest hindrances to peace, is our inability to be silent. For every situation in which we decide to hold our tongue or mind our own business, there are others where we let our heads be turned and join the chatter. We are constantly robbing ourselves of peace, because we choose to meddle in the affairs of others. We talk. We gossip.

Many people seem to regard silence as a trapping of an unnecessarily severe life – something for monks or nuns, for 'religious' people. It is true that in many religious orders, members observe periods of silence. But why should this be seen in a negative light? Silence can relieve us of the burden of having to respond. It can help us to avoid getting worked up over petty things.

Writer Max Picard points out that silence, 'Stands outside the world of profit and utility. It cannot be exploited; you cannot get anything out of it. It is "unproductive"; therefore it is regarded as useless. Yet there is more help and healing in silence than in all the useful things.'

Sometimes silence requires physical solitude. Personally, I think it is important to make time for solitude every day, even if only for a few minutes. My wife and I take a quiet walk in the morning as often as we can, and find it a good way to focus our thoughts. One elderly couple I know take a short walk before dinner every day, simply to be quiet together and enjoy the evening.

If we live or work closely with others – in a close-knit family, business or community, for instance – it is especially necessary to find times to be quiet and alone. Dietrich Bonhoeffer, who founded a small religious community in Northeast Germany in 1935 and was hanged by the Nazis ten years later for his part in the July 1944 attempt on Hitler's life, said that those who cannot live in community cannot live with themselves. But the reverse is just as true. Those who cannot live with themselves cannot live in community.

When we are alone, outward silence is easy to cultivate. (Inwardly, we may not be quiet at all, but may be buzzing with ideas and plans.) When we are with others, it becomes more difficult. Silence involves more than not talking – it means learning to listen.

Not to react, not to revise or embellish or expound, not even to respond, but simply to *listen* is a gift. As Mother Teresa of Calcutta once pointed out: 'All our words are useless if they do not come from within.'

All of us know what it is like to sit with someone we love, not saying anything yet feeling perfectly at ease. But silence is not always a source of peace. Sometimes even a slight pause in a conversation is enough to unsettle and embarrass us, and we grope for a quick reply to bridge the uncomfortable gap. When

drained

things are not right inside – when we are not at peace with ourselves, or not comfortable in the presence of another person – silence can even be frightening.

Recently, a friend told me how hard she finds it to drop everything that occupies her thoughts – the clamour of work, the distraction of plans, worries about tomorrow – and become inwardly still:

> It seems that when you are not at peace with yourself, you will have a hard time coping with blank spaces, either visually (nothing to watch or read), auditorily (nothing to listen to or hear), or physically (nothing to do, or the inability to do anything). You try to keep yourself distracted from the trouble inside – pain, conflicting goals, fear, accusations, whatever – but you only become more flustered.

Sophie Loeber, a childhood friend of my father's whom I have known all my life, recently wrote to me in a similar vein. 'I have often had to fight for peace in my life,' she says, 'but silence helped me turn inward.'

In 1937 the German religious community where Sophie lived was raided and dissolved by the Gestapo (the Nazi secret police). After rounding them up, lining the men against a wall and locking the women and children in a room, the police interrogated them and announced that they had twenty-four hours to leave the premises and get out of the country. Sophie remembers:

> When the Nazis forced us to leave our beloved home in the Rhön hills, we were not allowed to take anything with us other than the clothes on our backs. But we carried our treasures – joys and sorrows, struggles and times of celebration, and everything we had experienced there over many years – in our hearts. No

one could take those from us, even if we were utterly stripped of all material goods. That filled me with a silent joy and brought peace to my heart.

Many years later Sophie and her husband, Christian, lost two sons to a rare disease. First the boys went blind; then they became mentally debilitated. Both died in their teens, only a few years apart. Sophie was stricken beyond words. Questions tortured her, but gradually they gave way to a silence in which she found the strength to go on – and peace:

> Again and again I asked myself: why this terrible trial? Sometimes the discouragement seemed too much to bear. Yet later, in times when I was able to collect my thoughts and become inwardly silent, I realized that my concerns were much too small, too personal. Christian and I had been circling around our own needs, forgetting that there were people right next door who had needs too.

More recently, Sophie lost her husband to cancer, and then a third son (married, with children) in an electrical accident. Yet she will still tell you that not only has her suffering taught her to become quiet, but also 'to let go of everything that ties us down'. Inner silence and detachment, she says, have made her better able to respond to the pain of others.

Perhaps the 'letting go' that Sophie refers to is what seventeenth-century Quaker William Penn (after whom Pennsylvania is named) meant when he set down these words of advice: 'Love silence even in the mind; for thoughts are to that as words to the body, troublesome. True silence is the rest of the mind, and is to the spirit what sleep is to the body, nourishment and refreshment.'

drained

3 Let Go

To surrender to too many demands,
to commit oneself to too many projects,
to want to help everyone in everything
is to succumb to violence.

THOMAS MERTON

The best way not to experience peace of mind is to focus continually on yourself. Some people seem inclined to watch themselves constantly, as if in a mirror. They make themselves unnecessarily tense – and wind up completely drained. Others may not be so conscious of their inner state, but they are just as tense because they cannot let go of old hurts. With one it may be a smouldering resentment; with another an unfulfilled desire or an unconquered frustration.

Winifred went through a period of deep grief after her only son was stillborn. Unable to let go of her loss, she clung to the idea that she must have done something wrong to bring it about, even though her doctor assured her this could not have been the case. Only years later was she able to stop torturing herself. By sharing with someone else the full details of everything she imagined she had done wrong, she was able to let go of her self-accusations.

Winifred's long inner conflict points to a source of anxiety that causes many people heartache: their attempt to come to terms with a tragedy they feel responsible for. Whether or not they objectively bear guilt, the key to resolving it is letting go. Self-recrimination never brings healing but leads to unhealthy introspection.

For some, another source of inner frustration is their inability to relinquish the control they try to exert over others. As a family counsellor, I have seen how crippling this can be in the home, especially when it defines the relationship between a parent and child. In many homes, a great deal of unpeace, particularly between older teenagers (or even adult children) and parents, could be solved if parents were able to let go of their children and not fret incessantly over them or pressure them with plans for their future. My mother, a teacher, used to tell parents, 'The greatest disservice you can do your children is to chain them to yourselves. Let go of them.'

Emotional ties can create tensions outside the home, too. The tendency to meddle, advise or criticize others runs countless people to a frazzle and makes life miserable for everyone around them.

Molly Kelly, a friend who is known for her expertise in teenage sexuality, has valuable insights on the search for peace of mind – and the role of letting go in finding it.

I grew up in a Catholic family with five brothers and a sister, and Mom and Dad loved us very much. Not everything always went right, but love was the glue that bound us together. I went off to college and met the love of my life: Jim, a handsome young medical student at Georgetown University. Ours was a marriage made in heaven, as they say. He loved me, I loved him. Over the next eleven years, we were blessed with eight children.

Then one day, twenty-two years ago, my life changed forever. Jim and I were away for the weekend with our best friends. It wasn't easy to get away because of Jim's schedule at the hospital, and because of our children. So we were very excited. We were going to spend the weekend at a winter resort in the Pocono Mountains of Pennsylvania. But let me now fast-forward you to the event that catapulted me into an unrest and sadness that permeated every fibre of my being and remained there for years...

I was at the top of a sled run, chatting with our friends, when I noticed a commotion at the bottom of the slope. Jim had just gone down the hill on the sled, but I hadn't watched him so I didn't know it had anything to do with him. I saw several people waving to us, and I wondered what was going on. Then someone yelled for me to come down quickly because Jim had been hurt. I ran the whole way down the hill, slipping and falling and getting up again, and when I arrived at the scene there was a crowd around Jim. They stepped aside and made room for me, and I knelt at his side. He was semi-conscious and bleeding profusely. I'll skip the details and get to the end. Jim died.

I was devastated. Jim was my best friend, my pillow-talk buddy, the father of our children, the builder of our dreams. I couldn't begin to fathom life without him. I will never forget going home and hugging each one of the children, who had already been told that their dad had died. Our eldest, Jim, was twelve, and our youngest, Dan, was fourteen months. The older ones were pale, sad and clinging to each other. The younger ones weren't sure what was going on. The house was filled with people, noise, and lots and lots of food. (It's interesting how people bring food to console a grieving family.) We were shielded and surrounded with family and good friends, and I was grateful for the outpouring of love, but I was too hurt to thank anyone. I was wounded and bleeding just like Jim, and no one could fix my wounds either, so they seeped and festered for years.

I was able to go on as far as taking care of the kids was concerned because I loved them so much, and because I promised myself I would never dishonour Jim's memory by doing a shabby job of raising our children. I still had two in nappies, and because children want things to be better quickly, the rest of them went back to playing football in the living room, making a playhouse out of my sofa cushions, and making demands on my time and patience. Time I had; in fact it weighed heavily on me, even though I never seemed to get done all that I had to do. Each day dragged on, and I couldn't wait for bedtime so I could go to sleep and forget for just a little while that Jim had died. I was short on patience.

I was never alone, yet I was lonely beyond belief. It was only later, when peace came, that I discovered the difference between loneliness and being alone. I still dread loneliness, but I have come to cherish times when I am alone.

Some time after her husband's death, Molly took up an issue that had concerned him greatly: abortion. As a Catholic physician who believed in the sacredness of all life, Jim had been an ardent critic of abortion, and Molly shared his views.

I began by addressing the issue in classes at local Catholic high schools, and within a few years I was speaking quite a bit. I arranged my schedule so that I would be home when the kids got back from school in the afternoon.

After a while I realized that I wasn't getting to the heart of the problem. I realized I needed to talk about the root of abortion, which had to do with unwanted pregnancies, which had to do with casual sex. So I began to speak about sexual responsibility. The invitations to speak came pouring in. I was asked to speak in so many schools and so many other venues that I became overwhelmed and didn't know where to turn.

Friends suggested that I cut down on my speaking, but I felt called to it, and I wasn't about to give it up. Still, something had to give. It was then that I realized that what had to give was *me*.

I liked to be in control. I was the mother of eight children, and I ran a tight ship. I bought the food, I made the dinners, I washed the clothes, I helped with the homework, I went to the plays and ball games, I was home and school president. The word 'surrender' was not in my vocabulary. What I didn't realize was that surrender does not mean giving up so much as it means giving over. I had to give over my control, my unrest, my loneliness, my being overwhelmed – even my children – and let Someone stronger than me take the reins. And in each area of my life where I was able to do this, the tangible peace I experienced was almost instantaneous.

Molly has found this realization of her own limitations and letting go of what she cannot handle vital in her role as a speaker. She has spoken to more than a million teenagers – 'my favourite people in the whole world' – and to thousands and thousands of parents. She addressed a gathering of six thousand priests in Rome, and a meeting of fifty cardinals and bishops in California.

My schedule can be overwhelming, but it no longer overwhelms me. My peace is deep. It's a serenity that seems to have settled in for the long haul, for as long as I keep renewing my surrender. I say yes to speaking engagements when I can, and I say no when I can't. Am I always right? I doubt it. But I have come to realize that it is only in surrender that true peace will come.

Countless people struggle on bravely, even when they feel burnt out, simply because they are not willing to let down their guard. They are determined to steer their own lives, cost what it may.

Such people over-commit and then take days off to recuperate. They work at balancing their schedule, at discerning their priorities. They try to be kind and loving at home and patient at work. At the end of the day they still have no real peace.

Even with the best efforts, our strength is minuscule, and our solutions patchy. There is a real limit to what each of us can do. Acknowledging this makes it easier to let go of our problems and relinquish our need to solve every one of them our way. As Martin Luther King used to say, we are not so much independent as interdependent. When we realize this, we will discover that even the highest hurdle is no longer insurmountable.

El Salvador's Archbishop Oscar Romero, whose outspokenness on behalf of his country's exploited poor people earned him an assassin's bullet in 1980, was not born brave. In fact, he was appointed archbishop because both church authorities and the country's military leaders figured he was a safe bet – a conservative defender of the *status quo*. But three short years transformed Romero into a champion of human rights. Though he knew the meaning of self-doubt and hesitation, he chose to focus his sights on a cause greater than himself.

Romero would die without the satisfaction of seeing the positive changes that would eventually come in the condition of the people he was fighting for. But when, two weeks before his murder, a journalist asked him if he was afraid to die, Romero responded:

> If they kill me, I will rise again in the Salvadoran people. I tell you this without any boasting, with the greatest humility…. May my death be for the freedom of my people and as a witness to hope in the future. You can say, if they come to kill me, that I forgive and bless those who do it. Hopefully they may realize that they will be wasting their time. A bishop will die, but the people will never perish.

In the days and months following his death, these words proved true as one individual after another stepped forward to carry on the fight for human rights, joining forces in a struggle far greater than any one man. Romero was right: all any of us can do is to plant seeds, and then let go, trusting others to care for them so that one day they will flourish.

4 The Lost Art

Whoever opts for revenge
should dig two graves.

CHINESE PROVERB

The holiday had been long in coming. Enjoying the chance to relax, Bridie and Mick McGoldrick turned on the television in their small mobile home, near Warrenpoint, Northern Ireland, to catch the news. That day, July 8, 1996, a taxi driver had been shot through the head and murdered in Lurgan. The Loyalist paramilitaries who claimed responsibility for the killing, which took place in the little parish of Drumcree and was prompted by feuding over a march route, had apparently called for a taxi, knowing that its driver would almost certainly be a Catholic – and therefore a prime target. But when the news was first announced, neither Bridie nor Mick thought much of it, even though their only son, Michael, lived in Lurgan and drove a taxi; if any relative of theirs had been involved, they would have been informed before, they reasoned. But a later newscast offered more information: Lurgan taxi driver, early thirties, married with one child, wife expecting another. At that, Mick and Bridie looked at each other. And then came the crunch: just graduated from Queen's University, Belfast, on Friday.

Michael McGoldrick was dead, and his parents knew it. Mick remembers:

> We both ran outside. I went down on my knees, and I hit the ground with my fists. I looked up to the sky and cried out, 'Hanging on a cross was nothing to what we are going through.' I turned to my wife. 'Bridie,' I said, 'we'll never even smile again.' Michael was our only child. Michael was our world.
>
> Soon my family arrived and confirmed that it was indeed our son who had been murdered. We returned back home to Craigavon. That night we asked everyone to leave the house; Bridie and I had decided we would take our lives. We set the house in order, and then we showered and put on our pyjamas.
>
> I remember heading for the kitchen to get something to eat; I didn't want to take the tablets on an empty stomach. Friends and relatives had left the refrigerator full of things to eat – ham, turkey, chicken, cheese – but they hadn't left any butter. So I got two slices of bread and made a cooked-ham sandwich, with no butter. I came back into the living room and sat down on the settee beside Bridie. I took a bite out of the sandwich, and it stuck to the roof of my mouth. I turned and looked at Bridie. There I was, trying to get this bread from the roof of my mouth, and I just thought, aren't we two silly people? And the thought of suicide left us.
>
> The next day, Wednesday, we were down at Michael's wake. We thought our trouble was bad until we met a mother whose seventeen-year-old daughter had taken her own life some time before. There was a woman more troubled than we. And I remember the police called us in and an inspector said, 'Mr. McGoldrick, what has happened to you is the worst thing that could happen to any father.' I said, 'No, it isn't. The worst thing that could happen to me is my son coming home and telling me

he had murdered that taxi driver.' That was the truth.

On Thursday, Michael was to be buried. So before they put the lid on his coffin someone said, 'Do you want to say a final farewell to your son?' And I said, 'Yes.' I went up the stairs to where my son was lying in his coffin. I put my hands on top of his hands, and I said, 'Goodbye, son, I'll see you in heaven.' And all of a sudden I felt a great sense of power come over me, giving me strength. I didn't know what it was at the time, but I know now. I remember that someone said to me, 'We don't think you're fit to help carry the coffin.' And I said, 'Yes I am. I'll carry my son's coffin on his final journey.'

I knew the television cameras would be at the graveside – they always are in this country – and I wanted to give them a message. I wrote on a piece of paper: 'Bury your pride with my son,' and on the bottom I added, 'Forgive them.' There at my son's grave, I spoke that message on camera: 'I forgive them, my family forgives them.'

It was that simple, really. Despite the tremendous pain of losing our son, Bridie and I knew we had to forgive. Once we decided to go on, not to kill ourselves, we knew forgiveness was our only option. Otherwise we would have been consumed by our own bitterness.

Before Michael's murder, I'd never been one for going to church – I used to go to Mass, but only to make Bridie happy. But when Michael died, my life changed. In many different ways I felt the nearness of God, and my heart responded. That feeling of nearness has never left me, and it's what keeps me going today. Through forgiving my son's murderers, my life was turned around 180 degrees.

Despite the intensity of her pain, Bridie also refused to let anger overcome her. The initial shock left her reeling in disbelief: why would anybody hurt my child? She recalls:

Michael wasn't even born in Northern Ireland. He was Scottish, like me; and it was obvious by his accent. The pain I went through – it's a pain only another mother who's lost her son can understand. I was in another world, just sort of watching everything as it happened. None of it was happening to me.

But through all our tears and grief, we were given the strength to forgive. I remember getting ready to go to Mass one morning when suddenly I burst into tears. I said to Mick, 'Did I not love your child enough?' And he said, 'What do you mean?' I said, 'Mick, why have I no anger, why have I no hatred toward those that killed him?' And he said, 'Well Bridie, I don't know. That's a gift from God.' We both felt that we had to mean what we said when we prayed the Lord's Prayer: 'Forgive us our trespasses as we forgive those who trespass against us.'

All of Michael's life, he was loved and wanted. To bring anger or hatred in now, I felt, would be destroying my son, destroying our love for him. I would be saying that love was wrong.

Mick and Bridie now pour their energy into running United Christian Aid, a charity that collects, sorts and packages clothing and household items, which are then sent to Romania for distribution to people in need. In the faces of the Romanian children, many of whom are orphans, the McGoldricks see their own son's face reflected time and again. But the charity does more than send much-needed aid to Romania. It provides aid of a different sort to the people of Northern Ireland, as well: through giving, people come to realize that the need of others is greater than their own, and Mick and Bridie have watched as Catholics and Protestants form friendships across sectarian divides.

Before Michael's death, the McGoldricks would rarely venture beyond the Catholic area in which they live. Today, there's no place, no community, they won't visit. Often they are asked to attend gatherings and tell their story, and they never turn down the chance to speak about forgiveness. As Mick says:

There's an awful lot of sectarianism in this country, divisions of Catholics and Protestants who are at loggerheads with one another. They're all supposedly Christian, but if you came down from Mars, you'd begin to wonder. But the people going at each other, that's all you ever hear about from the media. There's not enough coverage here of the forgiveness of people, the goodness of people. They don't tell you that Catholics and Protestants are praying together, but it's true, and it's happening more and more.

You know, when you look at Northern Ireland's problems in comparison to the need in the Third World and in Eastern Europe, it kind of fades into the background. What greater way of bringing Northern Ireland together than sharing what we have with people less fortunate? That's what we are trying to do through this charity. And that's what we aim to keep on doing, regardless of what happens here.

If politicians want to talk about peace, fine. But peace isn't just something you can make by talking. You have to work for it. And I still say that only people with peace within their hearts can speak of peace, otherwise they're speaking about something that they know absolutely nothing about. You can only speak about peace when you have experienced it in your heart. I can speak of peace because I know what peace is, and it comes when we forgive and when we are forgiven.

Most of us do not have to deal directly with murder; and many of the things we obsess over are even laughable by comparison. Still we may have a hard time forgiving. Especially if our resentment has grown over a long period, it will take time and effort to root out. And whether the hurt is real or imagined, it will eat away at us as long as we nurse it.

Human nature being what it is, the ability to see the goodness in every person we meet is rare. Even our relationships
with those who are closest to us are clouded now and then, if
only by petty grievances. True peace with others requires effort.
Sometimes it demands the readiness to give way, to let go or to
remain silent; at others, the willingness to be frank, or the courage to confront or speak out. One thing remains constant, however: if we want peace in our relationships, we must be willing
to forgive over and over.

In 1988, on a visit to Israel, I met Elias Chacour for the first
time. A Palestinian priest frequently nominated for the Nobel
Peace Prize and known throughout the world for his tireless
efforts for the cause of reconciliation and peace in his homeland, he is a man who might justifiably be expected to harbour
bitterness. In 1947 his village was destroyed, its inhabitants
driven out. Elias has been imprisoned more than once and
endured years of harassment at the hands of the Israeli government. But this 'man without a country' remains one of the most
warm-hearted and compassionate people I know. Speaking of
forgiveness, he says:

> Why should I love those who have destroyed my home? Why
> should I love those who have tortured me? It is certainly a hard
> thing to love one's enemies. But if I am called to love my per-
> secutor, then I must do everything to remind him that he will
> never have any dignity unless he sees his own dignity in my face.
> This is not surrendering to your enemy, it is straightening your-
> self up and saying to your torturer: 'You have hurt me so much
> that I forgive you.' Don't go first to the one who is under the foot
> of the persecutor; go to the persecutor himself and tell him to let
> go, so that the one who is underfoot can get up and say, 'You are
> my brother, and I forgive you.'

Forgiving has nothing to do with being fair, or with excusing wrongdoing; in fact, it may mean pardoning someone for something inexcusable. (Ironically, those who suffer the worst things in life often forgive most readily.) When we excuse someone, we brush their mistake aside as if it were nothing. When we forgive someone, in contrast, there may be good reason to hold onto our hurt, but we let go of it anyway. We refuse to seek revenge. Our forgiveness may not always be accepted, yet the act of reaching out our hand in reconciliation saves us from anger and indignation. Even if we remain wounded, a forgiving attitude will prevent us from lashing back at someone who has caused us pain. And it can strengthen our resolve to forgive again the next time we are hurt.

Not that we should swallow our hurts. To the contrary, people who push their grievances down into their subconscious in an attempt to forget them only cripple themselves. Before we can forgive a hurt, we must be able to face it. Sometimes, of course, it may not be possible (or helpful, even if it is possible) to confront the person we are struggling to forgive, and then the best solution is to share our pain with someone else we trust. Once we have done this, we must let go. Otherwise we may remain resentful forever, waiting for an apology that never comes.

Naturally we must seek to be forgiven, too. Each of us has been hurt at one time or another, and each of us has hurt others. And therefore, just as all of us must forgive, so all of us need to be forgiven. Without forgiveness, we will not find peace. After all, regardless of how 'good' we're tempted to think we are, none of us is perfect. A legend about Brother Angelo, a monk in St. Francis of Assisi's order, illustrates the problem beautifully.

On Christmas Eve, Brother Angelo cleans his simple mountain hut and decorates it for Mass. He says his prayers, sweeps the hearth, hangs a kettle over the fire and then sits back to wait for St. Francis, whom he expects later in the day. Just then three outlaws appear at the door, begging for food. Frightened and angry, Brother Angelo sends them away empty-handed, scolding and warning them that thieves are damned to hellfire.

When Francis arrives, he senses that something is not right. Brother Angelo then tells him about his visitors, and Francis sends him up into the mountains with a jug of wine and a loaf, to find them and ask their forgiveness. Brother Angelo is indignant. Unlike Francis, he cannot see the wild men as brothers –only as outlaws. He sets out obediently, however, and by night- fall, having followed the men's footsteps in the snow, he finds them and makes amends. Some time later, the legend goes, they leave their cave and join the order.

drained

5 Get Real

The hardest thing is facing yourself. It's easier to shout
'Revolution' and 'Power to the people' than it is to look at
yourself and try to find out what's real inside you and
what isn't. When you're pulling the wool over your own
eyes—that's the hard one.

JOHN LENNON

I f someone asked me to pick the most fundamental require-
ment for inner peace, I would probably say honesty. Whether
taken to mean truthfulness in a general sense, or knowledge
of one's condition, or the ability to call a spade a spade, or
the willingness to admit failure in front of others, honesty is a
basic premise for peace. We may strive and struggle for peace
until our dying breath, but we will never find it as long as we
are unwilling to place ourselves under the clear light of truth.
Dishonesty is one of the greatest impediments along the path to
peace, because it prevents us from finding a square footing on
which to base our search.

Thomas Merton suggested we must, 'Become conscious that
the person we think we are, here and now, is at best an impostor
and a stranger. We must constantly question his motives and
penetrate his disguises.' Otherwise our attempts at self-knowledge are bound to fail. Shakespeare understood this too:

This above all: To thine own self be true
And it must follow, as the night the day,
Thou canst not then be false to any man.

Of course, this is easier said than done. A friend of mine, Jean-
ette, recently told me how, as a young woman, she had looked
for peace year after year – in labour movements and political
organizations, university groups and co-operatives and communities – but had neglected the vital task of tending to the
tensions in herself. Like countless others, her seeking bore fruit
only once she was able to come to terms with the true state of
her life by looking within, deeply and honestly.

But self-knowledge is only the first step. By itself it will not
bring us peace or fulfilment, and may even lead us away from it
by trapping us in a downward spiral of self-concern. Often, the
end result is hypocrisy; life becomes an act. And perhaps those
most at risk of this are the ones who go to such lengths to be
seen as 'good people'.

At one time or another, we have all put up fronts, attempting
to appear before others in a pleasing light. In the theatre of
ancient Greece, actors wore masks to portray characters. By
changing masks, an actor could quickly switch from one role
to another. In fact, the Greek word for 'actor' gives us the English word 'hypocrite'. In the same way, each of us has masks we
sometimes wear. In short, we all take our turn at playing the
hypocrite.

To realize who we really are means to face issues we have
previously avoided, and to let ourselves be confronted. Un-
fortunately, most of us do not take the first step, let alone the
second, because we fear that changes may be demanded of us.
We are reluctant to give up the comfort of self-satisfaction, and
so we attempt to convince ourselves that nothing is amiss, that

drained

everything is going fine. If only we recognized how much deeper and greater the peace is that comes from living with a fully awakened awareness of our true inner state!

Sylvia, now in her nineties, was pursuing a promising music career in London, just before the outbreak of the Second World War. A committed left-wing idealist, she, like many others of her generation, participated enthusiastically in the peace movement of her youth. But the inconsistent attitude of many 'pacifists' – an opposition to killing, but not to social injustice – dissatisfied her and left her wanting something more:

> My husband, Raymond, and I met regularly with a group of friends and discussed ideas. We searched and searched to find a way through the labyrinth of human ideas – war, peace, politics, conventional morals versus free love, etc – but came no nearer to finding a peaceful or just society.

Later, during the long, difficult birth of her first child, it dawned on Sylvia that her personal life was marked by the very same troubles she was fighting in society. Despite the glowing prospects for her future in music, her marriage was in shambles and her mind in turmoil. To put it bluntly, she felt drained. Then and there she decided that before she could contribute anything to world peace, she needed to take an honest look at her own life, to find peace within herself and with others.

Living with inconsistency can become a habit. Once we are used to it, we may soon become insincere, and then downright deceitful as well. When this happens, it will take a concerted effort to strip away the falsehoods we have been hiding behind and to become honest again, both with ourselves and with those we have been deceiving. As my father once put it: 'Complete peace demands complete honesty. Let us be genuine and say what we think, even if we are off the mark, rather than use the right words without meaning them. We cannot live in peace with others unless truth is in our hearts.'

Looking back at conversations I have had with people experiencing times of upheaval, I can say that the battle between truth and deceit is always a hard one to fight, especially when someone has been deluded into believing that honesty is too high a price to pay for inner peace. Such people may not even feel the need to fight things through at first, because they have blinded themselves so completely to the fact that they have been living a lie.

In *The Brothers Karamazov,* the great Russian novelist Dostoevsky gives us just such a character: Fyodor Pavlovitch, an old man who mockingly asks Father Zossima what he must do to gain eternal life. The priest begins by telling him to avoid the pitfalls of loose living, then adds this wisdom:

> Above all, don't lie to yourself. The man who lies to himself and listens to his own lie comes to such a pass that he cannot distinguish the truth within or around him, and so loses all respect for himself and for others. Having no respect, he ceases to love, and in order to occupy and distract himself without love he gives way to passions and coarse pleasures, and sinks to bestiality in his vices, all from continually lying to other men and to himself. The man who lies to himself can be more easily offended than anyone. You know that nobody has insulted him, but that he has invented the insult for himself, has lied and exaggerated to make it picturesque, has caught at a word and made a mountain out of a molehill. He knows that himself, yet he will be the first to take offence, and will revel in his resentment till he feels great pleasure in it, and so pass on to genuine vindictiveness.

If we are truly determined to find peace of heart, there is always a solution: to admit our weaknesses, failings and wrongdoings

drained

to another person. Once we have recognized the disharmony between our true character and the side of ourselves we present to others, we will remain painfully aware of the tension until we can reconcile the two. Even if we mend our ways and turn away from past wrongs, we cannot experience full peace of mind until we are willing to share our secret burdens with another person.

Ann's search for happiness, fulfilment and peace went on year after year – until she finally stopped in her tracks and faced herself squarely.

I had everything a woman could want: a loving husband, four beautiful children, financial security and a home to call my own. Yet part of me was screaming inside: 'I don't want "everything". There must be more to life than a nice spouse and children, a comfortable home, affluence.' I grew desperate and scared. Why was I so unhappy?

I was raised in a home that looked pretty good on the outside. My mother and father worked hard, Dad as a factory worker and Mum as a housewife. People thought well of us, and no one knew the hell we were already perishing in.

Nobody knew, for instance, that I was sexually abused by my older brother for three years, starting when I was six. Nobody knew how my unstable teenage sister was beaten by my father with a belt in front of the whole family, simply because he could not cope with her and let his temper get the better of him. Nobody knew how a small thing such as spilling your milk at the dinner table was enough to put Dad into a rage that might last as long as two hours.

We lived in fear of making a mistake, of making Dad mad. After all, he drank a six-pack of beer or more every night when he came home from work, and a whole case on the weekend. If

37

get real

he lost his temper after that, which happened several evenings a week, there was little any of us could do, including Mum, who sat there and bore it all silently. All evening long he would go on with his tirades, calling my mother one foul obscenity after another, and banging his fist on the table.

Later, at night, we would sometimes hear him start up again, yelling because my mother was not interested in 'intimacy'. We children would run for our rooms and put pillows over our heads, leave the house and go find a friend to hang out with, or turn up the volume on the TV. We were scared, bewildered, confused, and there was nothing to do but block out Dad's anger.

One thing I did to escape all the pain was sing. I used to sing and sing. I sang so much that my brothers and sisters would get very annoyed. 'Well, at least I'm not fighting,' I would say. I didn't realize it then, of course, but my songs were an outlet for my anxiety. I felt unloved and wanted so much to be loved. I thought: if I could be good and behave, others would be happy. If only there were peace in my family, I would be happy. When I was older I felt I couldn't do anything right, and that I wasn't worth much anyway. Things got worse in my teenage years, and I got involved in all the usual things. The worst was that it was all hidden: the needs of my childhood, the misdeeds of adolescence...

On the outside I was a normal, decent, even religious young woman. Yet on the inside there was turmoil and darkness. My life was one big lie. When I married, I half thought the problems might solve themselves, but they just carried on. Like my childhood and youth, my marriage looked fine from a distance, but to be honest, it was a mess.

When I was a little girl, my despair would drive me to pray for help. Not that I expected God to do anything. I didn't really think he loved me. I was bad, and I was convinced God wouldn't love someone like me. The more I wanted to be loved and cared for, the harder I grew, and the less capable of accepting love.

Now, as a married woman with a growing family, I still had no peace. I had known self-doubt and self-hatred for a long time, but I began to project those feelings on everyone else. I hated the whole world. I was angry, and I felt rejected and worthless. I was an emotional wreck.

More than anything, I needed freedom from the pain of my past, but I looked for it in all the wrong places. To be honest, I was looking for one thing, and I went after it with a desperate passion: I wanted to be loved. I looked for love in my husband, Bob, but I felt he didn't measure up; I looked for it in my friends, and they also failed. I looked for it in God, too. Somehow it remained outside my grasp. I could not feel love or experience it.

Then, during a sort of retreat several years ago, Bob and I tried to consider the course of our lives. It was a healing process, but very painful at the time, for it led us to the hard recognition that our marriage was a mess. We came to realize that we needed to face each other honestly, once and for all.

It was during this difficult period that I found peace. But first I had to make the humiliating discovery that I was a completely self-centred person, hell-bent on my own happiness; and further, that I was full of hatred toward my husband, who I thought had failed me and who couldn't provide the love I so desperately needed and wanted. True, Bob had failed me in many ways, but I now saw that I was an emotional leech. For years I had been sapping what love he did have, and causing him to retreat. In short, the problem was me. Finally I could admit that my self-obsession was the main cause of my misery.

As I had when I was younger, I asked God to help me, but this time I believed he would. Suddenly I was able to feel remorse for the hurts I had caused others, instead of feeling sorry for myself and worrying about how others had hurt me. For the first time in my life, I even felt a desire to forgive those who had hurt me, especially my father. I felt remorse toward God, too, and in return I felt his love. I felt acceptance and forgiveness.

As Bob and Ann began to talk things over, they saw each other as never before. They were able to forgive each other for everything that had made their marriage miserable, and move on. Ann continues:

> I do not always have the feeling of peace. I still struggle with feelings of anxiety at times, or lapse into old worries and fears. I still have to work at being my true self, to fight the temptation to please people or gain their approval. But there is fulfilment in doing things for others. It doesn't matter what it is. Some days I find happiness in babysitting or housekeeping; other days in preparing a meal for someone or doing their laundry. I am grateful whenever I get a chance to care for an elderly person.
>
> I still have scars, I'm sure, but I am accepted as I am. In being able to use my energy to help others, rather than focusing on myself, I have received a gift I never found while seeking it for myself: pure joy.

Revealing our true colours, even (or perhaps especially) to someone we love and trust, is always a painful exercise. But as we shall see later in this book, there is no way around it. If we want to find peace, we must be ready to accept its cost, dear as it may be. To seek cheap peace is to chase a will-o'-the-wisp; the attempt is both foolish and exhausting.

Peace can be lost in a moment – through stubbornness or deceit, pride, self-will or the false comfort of an easy way out. Yet it is never too late to start looking for it again, even if it has eluded us for years. Whenever we are able to take an honest look at ourselves – 'warts and all' – it should not be hard to refocus on our need for peace.

6 Burn Your Fingers (Again)

Trust the physician, and drink his remedy
in silence and tranquillity:
For his hand, though heavy and hard, is guided
by the tender hand of the Unseen,
And the cup he brings, though it burn your lips,
has been fashioned of the clay which the Potter
has moistened with his own sacred tears.

KAHLIL GIBRAN

From childhood on we are taught that it is dangerous to trust, and in a way this is true. To trust involves taking risks. Trust means giving others the benefit of the doubt. It requires the willingness to make oneself vulnerable. But the distrust we learn as children, as a way of protecting ourselves from harm, can be our undoing as adults. We learn to keep others out, to avoid jeopardy. The isolation this breeds can be fatal, because without trust we can neither share nor love.

Contrary to popular opinion, trust is not the same as weak-willed naiveté. It does not require us to go through life unperturbed and happy, pretending that nothing is wrong and taking everything at face value. Such 'trust' would be suicidal in today's climate. Yet the alternatives – anxiety, mistrust and suspicion – are equally deadly. Mennonite writer Daniel Hess notes:

It does not matter that many workers are covered by health insurance, that the forty-hour work week provides time for leisure, that salaries give some of us a degree of affluence, and that science goes a long way in making tools safe and in predicting volatile nature. In spite of all that, we are anxious.

People have tight stomachs and sweaty palms because of learned habits of nervous busyness, fear of what could happen, panic brought on by addictions, depressions from chemical imbalances, too many masters and too many commitments, and desires unfulfilled.

Many are anxious in their relationships, stressed by friction and diminished by betrayals. They suffer from all-too-real fears of legal actions, unfair competition, downsizing, and hostile take-overs.

Sadly, the betrayals, the gossip and the backbiting that are an inevitable part of everyday life keep many people from ever daring to trust. Clare, a one-time businesswoman who now dedicates much of her time to caring for an elderly neighbour, writes:

> As an impediment to peace, mistrust is a biggie. We may try to defend ourselves and those we love by being wary, but we end up building walls of suspicion. If someone takes advantage of us or acts unfairly, we jump to assume the worst – and not just for that particular situation, but from then on. We see trust's cousin, vulnerability, as a sign of weakness, something stupid or simplistic.
>
> When we refuse to trust others, we may think we are protecting ourselves, but the opposite is true. Love is the greatest protection, the deepest security. When we are mistrustful, we can neither give nor receive love. We cut ourselves off from God and from each other.

At the community I call home, the Bruderhof, as in any close-knit group of people, the proximity of our homes and the visibility of everyone's day-to-day life create an enormous potential

for tensions caused by frustration, speculation or gossip.
Yet from the very start of our communal life seventy-five years
ago, we have found that a mutual commitment to 'open speaking' can maintain genuine trust and peace. A statement drawn
up in the 1920s by our movement's first members contains
these lines:

> There must never be talk, either in open remarks or by insinu-
> ation, directed against anyone, or against their individual char-
> acteristics – and under no circumstances behind their backs.
> Gossiping in one's family is no exception. An open word spoken
> directly to another person deepens friendship and will not be
> resented.

Ellen still remembers her excitement on reading this for the
first time – and realizing that it was actually practised:

> When I discovered that there would be no gossip – no talking
> about anyone behind their back – it was like an enormous weight
> slipping off my shoulders. Where I came from, gossip was a way
> of life. Like anyone, I worried about what people thought and
> said of me behind my back, but I hadn't really looked at those
> worries closely and realized what an awful burden they were;
> how much they can affect your life year after year. And now: to
> know that if someone felt something wrong in me, they would
> come and tell me – it was like new ground under my feet.

All too often our relationships with others are broken because
we lack this trust. For whatever reason, justifiable or not, we do
not dare to believe that we will be loved just as we are, with all
our shortcomings and foibles. But that is just what we must do.
Rather than frittering away our lives in fear and mistrust, our
attitude should be one of willingness to trust others repeatedly – even those who betray us.

How to find this level of trust? There is no easy method, no guaranteed equation. But one thing seems certain: the level at which we trust is directly linked to the view we hold of ourselves. If we insist on placing a greater value on our own opinions than those of others, we should not wonder if trusting seems difficult. Our human nature does not endorse the virtue of humility; it runs counter to every survival instinct we have. Humility requires more than just a gentle demeanour: it demands the willingness to be vulnerable, to be hurt. As a result, of all the stepping stones toward peace, humility may be the hardest to comprehend – and to accept.

There is plenty one could write about humility and its role in building trust, but there is no substitute for simply practising it from day to day. For it is only through actually opening ourselves up to others and trusting them that we discover the hidden blessings of vulnerability. And only through accepting our insignificance will we learn to welcome the peace that letting go of our self-importance brings. In the words of Malcolm Muggeridge:

> Power is the greatest snare of all. How terrible is power in all its manifestations – the voice raised to command, the hand stretched out to seize, the eyes burning with appetite. Money had better be given away; organizations had better be disbanded; bodies had better lie separately. There is no peace at all, except in looking across time at eternity beyond – as one looks at a distant view from a mountain top.

We will never find lasting peace unless we learn to trust, and we will never completely learn to trust until we have discovered humility. Yet though we would be foolish to expect these qualities to flourish in us overnight, they are powerful instruments of peace, well worth the effort it takes to master them.

Writer Dale Aukerman knows all too well what it is not to be in control, and it may seem that he has every right to protest the hand life has dealt him. The cancer he has been battling for years may get the better of him at any time. But he is at peace. His peace is not rooted in a weak resignation to the fact that he may soon die; his love for life remains undiminished, and he will surely go down fighting. Yet his closeness to death does not unnerve him or unbalance him. He finds that his trust in a higher power gives him continual strength and an even keel.

On November 5, 1996, I found out that I had a tumour three and a half inches across on my left lung. Later tests showed that the cancer had spread to the liver, the right hip and two spots in the spine. I learned that I could figure on living two to six months, with a median survival prospect of four months. It's amazing the reorientation of outlook that can come when you find out that you may have only a couple of months to live. Each day and each close relationship became more precious than before. Every morning I would think which day of the month it was – another day given to me by God. With fresh intentness I gazed at my family, my home, and the beauty of nature, know-ing that my time for seeing all this might very soon be at an end.

When my sister Jane died of an especially lethal form of cancer at the age of fourteen, my mother saw this as God's will: God chose to take her, and who were we as human beings to challenge that? For some people this type of view gives comfort. I see such things somewhat differently. I don't think God sends cancer or heart disease. When a drunken driver swerves into another car and kills a number of persons, I don't believe that is God's will. So much in the world is not what God intended and not what God wants.

After six cycles of chemotherapy, a regimen of nutritional supplements, and so much praying by a host of friends, I had another CAT scan, which showed that the tumour on my lung had shrunk to less than one-fourth of its earlier size. Two of the doctors spoke of that as a miracle.

Throughout my adult life I have been much involved in peacemaking, and during these past months I've especially cherished verses from the Bible about peace. One, which I thought of as I was being thrust in and out of an MRI tunnel, is from St. Paul's letter to the Philippians: 'The peace of God, which surpasses all understanding, will keep your hearts and your minds in Christ Jesus.'

This peace, as St. Paul understood it, is more than just tranquillity of spirit. It is wholeness of life and relationships that stands firm against all that tries to fragment and destroy us. It is a gift that can bear us up even when we walk through deep darkness.

7 Turn Around

Laying down your arms, surrendering, saying you are
sorry, realizing that you have been on the wrong track
and getting ready to start life over again from the
ground floor – that is the only way out of a hole.

C. S. LEWIS

Peace, as Sue understood it in 1972, simply meant an
end to the war in Vietnam. 'Growing up in the sixties,
I had no idea peace was anything deeper than that,'
she says. Born into middle-class America, Sue grew
up with every material thing she wanted. But by the end of
her teenage years, she was a desperate young woman, longing
for wholeness and peace in her life, yet so weighed down by
self-hatred and guilt, so drained, she felt at the end of her rope.

As one of four children of an often violent, alcoholic father, I
was part of a typical dysfunctional family – very middle class,
very unhappy. At the age of nine or ten I began toying with sex.
I noticed that if a boy in my neighbourhood 'wanted' me I had
power over him, and I began to use my looks to the fullest. I led
many boys and men on in this way without ever intending to
have sex with them. I just wanted to control them.

In 1968, at the age of fourteen, I found my sister and her husband dead in their apartment. Married for only three months to

a Navy man, this beautiful twenty-two-year-old woman's life was over. Was it a quarrel? Had he had a breakdown? Was it the fact that he was possibly headed for Vietnam? Only two dead bodies and a gun were left to tell the tale when my other sister and I walked in their door...

My life was thrown into utter confusion after this. Full of anger and hatred, especially toward my father, I began to lose myself in amphetamines, hashish and marijuana while getting drunk each weekend with a different man. By the time I was seventeen I had done just about everything, sexually. Ironically, some friends and I were part of the whole peace, love, anti-war thing that was so strong in those days. True, there was a great deal of idealism in the early 1970s, but the selfishness in many sex-lives was the opposite of the ideal.

For ten long years I struggled to find peace. But no matter how hard I fought or who tried to help me, I could not break out of the dark prison I had constructed for myself.

Eventually, though, it dawned on me that I could find freedom – if only I could lower my guard once and for all and reveal myself as the miserable person I was. I had to find someone I could trust and tell them my darkest secrets. I had to turn around, and then I would find the peace I had been seeking for so long.

In the next days my whole life flowed in front of my eyes; it was as if I saw every touch, look, word, thought that I had wallowed in, every person I had wilfully misled and hurt. With pain, but also with joy, I brought to light my blackest secrets, confiding in a female friend. I had to go back many times before I was able to get through everything. Peace poured into my heart after each cleansing. The years seemed to roll off me, and I felt free as a child again.

I'm over forty now, married, with children, but I feel much younger than I did at nineteen. And if someone asked me today what peace is, I could give them a far better answer.

All of us want to start again and to be changed – that is not the problem. The problem is: how? It is one thing to be humble, gentle or kind. But remorseful? To admit one's wrongs and feel truly sorry for them? To turn around? Harsh as it may seem, there is no peace without this. When a person takes responsibility for the things he or she has done wrong in life and turns around, a heart of stone becomes a heart of flesh, and every thought, every emotion, is transformed. A person's entire outlook changes.

It is easy enough to set a wrong right by means of an apology, or to shut an eye and gloss things over; people do this every day. While these measures may momentarily placate an uneasy conscience, they won't bring about lasting peace. Nor will the conventional approach of those psychologists or psychiatrists who tell people, 'You haven't done anything wrong; your behaviour is quite normal. You don't need to feel bad.' Lasting peace is not found by denying our failures, but by looking at them honestly and squarely.

Turning around does not mean self-torment; nor does it mean self-centred brooding or depression. But if it is real, the process will be painful. Gerald sought peace of mind unsuccessfully, year after year. Though deeply sorry for his past wrongdoings, he had never truly faced them square-on. He was a reliable, hard worker, but inside he was a tortured man. Behind the façade of his steady commitment to his family and his local church, he carried around with him the secret of an affair from his younger days, and a child from that relationship in a distant city.

In a time of crisis when he was approaching middle age, Gerald found himself confronting the true sum of his life up to that point. He says he knew there was no way he could 'make up for or undo' what he had done. Yet when he was able to feel the painful weight of his wrongdoing, he was filled with remorse, and went and apologized to every person he had let down or betrayed. Finally, he says, he was able to feel clean and whole.

Dramatic as his reckoning was, Gerald says that this experience, and the peace it brought him, was not a onetime event, but a process that continues to this day:

> Many times I thought I had finally found peace, only to realize that what I had found was merely a stepping stone, and that I had to go deeper. This will probably continue. Perhaps it is in the honest *pursuit* of peace that we find it.

THE IMPORTANCE of turning around is also shown in the story of my aunt Emy-Margret, a woman who has probably fought a harder fight in her search for peace of heart than anyone I know. When Emy-Margret, now in her late eighties, first met Hans, the man who later became her husband, she admired him – like everyone who knew him – for his intelligence, enthusiasm and charisma.

But what started as a happy marriage soon evolved into a nightmare. On the outside, things looked great: children arrived, one after the other, and the family seemed to enjoy a wholesome, harmonious life. Privately, however, Hans began to show a different side. He had an insatiable desire for personal power, and seemed willing to go any lengths to get it, no matter what the cost to others or himself.

Emy-Margret was initially troubled by her husband's manipulative style, but this didn't last for long. To criticize Hans meant to open herself to his sarcastic tongue-lashings, and it was much easier – more hassle-free, more comfortable – to accept him as he was. Not that this was entirely pleasant: Hans was mistrustful of almost everyone he lived or worked with, and there were few he hated more than his wife's family.

drained

But Emy-Margret's emotional dependence on her husband was so great that it blinded her to the deep wounds they inflicted on others; they simply trampled on anyone who got in their way or dared to oppose them. In effect, she became his accomplice, pandering to his ambitions. She remained strangely defensive of Hans – even after she discovered that he had been carrying on an affair with his secretary for years, and even after his tragic death in an air collision over France.

It was some time before Emy-Margret finally began to see that she had been living a lie; that everything she had hung on to – prestige, power and the attention of people who admired (or envied) her 'social standing' – had gained her no real happiness, but only personal devastation. During the following months, she underwent the agonizing process of sorting out the conflicting loyalties and emotions, pent-up lies and half-lies that had burdened her for decades. It was a long, intense battle, but she struggled to recognize her own guilt in supporting her husband's scheming and to put things right.

Twenty-five years have passed since then, and there is no question that my aunt's quest for peace has cost her much pain. She lost Hans without ever being reconciled to him, she embittered old friends who sided with her husband, and she estranged herself from several of her children in the process. Yet she assures me that in breaking her ties to her husband and turning around she has found a wholeness and healing she never knew before. As she wrote some years ago, 'Great liberation and peace was given to me and is still being given, far beyond my hopes and prayers.'

8 What You Really, Really Want

Until one is committed there is hesitancy,
the chance to draw back, always ineffectiveness.

W. H. MURRAY

Ashley Meaney had 'the look'. It set him apart from the friends of his youth in Melbourne. By the time he was nineteen, it had won him entry into Europe's fashion scene and placed him squarely in the ranks of the 'beautiful people'. His world revolved around the runways of Paris, Milan and London.

I was young. I'd made the scene. I was signed on by Elite, the best agency in the business. I was modelling in shows for the likes of Giorgio Armani. My image was being plastered on billboards. Things were certainly going great for a guy who not long before had been a class-A Aussie beach bum. Now I was riding the crest of a *real* wave, and I fully intended to ride this one as far as it would take me.

Modelling, I soon discovered, isn't just a job; it's a lifestyle. It becomes your life. Suddenly, a whole new world opened for me. There were night-clubs to frequent, with tables set aside just for models. Alcohol was free, drugs were free, sex was free – everything was there for the taking, and who was I to refuse?

Once, I found myself in Milan, strapped for cash and short on my rent. Hardly a problem: I simply did things like 'Dance for Dollars'. I'd be driven to a night-club and would spend the evening getting drunk and flirting with as many women as I possibly could, and then I'd be driven home. It was the club's way of attracting female business, and it paid well.

Often I'd be at a party and things would sort of blur towards the end, and without really knowing how I got there, I'd find myself in the home of some celebrity or other snorting cocaine all weekend. I was always willing to give something a try, even heroin.

Fame and power, personality and prestige, celebrity and fortune – those were my aspirations. That's the direction my wave was taking me. I put together a very, very good show that I called me. And it worked well. I was very popular; people enjoyed having me around. I was the down-to-earth, mad Aussie party guy. That was how I lived. That's how I did London, Paris, Milan.

In the late 1980s, New Age made its fashion-industry debut. White clothing became almost *de rigueur* as designers sought to infuse their work with a sense of spirituality. I began wearing an amethyst and spent a lot of time trying to astro-project. I read Buddhist literature and all the typical trendy stuff on dreams, and so on.

On August 20, 1989, the *Marchioness* went down in the Thames. The passenger launch was full of models and their agents, out for a night of partying on the river, when it collided with a larger boat. Fifty-seven people drowned. A lot of them were drugged out; it was that kind of party. One of the people who died was a very close friend of mine.

After that disaster, my search for meaning in life intensified. Nothing seemed very real; drinking and doing LSD and coke were the only things that made much sense to me. And then two months later my best friend in Australia died of an asthma attack... I had a lot of questions running through my mind, but no answers.

The day he died, I'd booked lunch with another model, Sibs (Cyrille, really, but everyone's always called her Sibs). We'd met in the park across from a popular restaurant. You couldn't smoke dope in the restaurant, so my friends and I would go into the park to enjoy a joint before dinner – grass on the grass we called it. And that's where I'd met her.

Well, we began dating and eventually moved to Paris together, both of us working as models. We both got into painting, and our modelling earned us enough to live on. We lived in a lovely apartment in Montmartre, a neighbourhood known for its artsy, alternative image, with some mystical elements blended in for good measure. And that's where we began to fall in love, I guess.

As our relationship deepened, I slowed down on the drug intake. But my search for peace was just getting more intense. And so I was reading mythology, and I was trying to meditate with crystals. And then a friend who was also attracted by New Age suggested I try the main religions as well. I'd not been to church as a child so I didn't know about the Old Testament or the New Testament; I didn't know much of anything about God, let alone Jesus. But my friend bought me a Bible, and I sat down at the table and opened it for the first time in my life.

What I read that day changed my life. I was overwhelmed with the feeling that God was real and that he cared about me. I felt this with my whole being, and it completely wowed me. My first reaction – and this shows where my heart was then – was: 'If I could put this in a cap, I'd be a millionaire tomorrow.' My drug mentality thought, this is better than any Ecstasy, any acid, any coke I've ever had.

This feeling of love, of peace – it was so new, so foreign to me. I knew it was what I'd been searching for, and what I knew so many others were searching for. Over the next several days,

I waited for the feeling to go away. But it never really left. It kept coming back, sometimes at very strange times or places. I'd be on the Metro in Paris, heading for a casting with my modelling portfolio tucked under my arm, and it would just come over me again. Warmth. Love. And it would reduce me to tears, right there on the train. Here I was, trying to be a model – you know, cool and hard and hip.

Sibs didn't quite know what to make of all this at first. She'd watched me try to astro-project and all that, so she assumed this was just another one of my 'trips'. She remained sceptical when I began making Christian friends and going to church – a place that at first completely petrified me, because I was completely out of my league and thus totally vulnerable. But the change that was taking place inside of me wasn't just a passing phase. When Sibs realized this, her curiosity eventually got the better of her, and she had to find out about God for herself. She did, all right.

Knowing that God was real gave my life a purpose. Not that everything happened overnight, but a seed had been planted, and change was inevitable. It became clear to me that my life was based on egocentric selfishness, that I had been the centre of a universe of my own design. That all had to be dismantled. My relationship with Sibs needed some drastic changes, too. Fortunately, we chose to stick together and to begin looking at each other with new eyes. We wanted our love to be enduring and unconditional. We stopped having sex, we stopped fighting, and we went through the painful process of quitting drugs. It was far from easy. We had been 'comfortable' with our dysfunctional relationship; now, all of a sudden, we were having to really relate. Amazingly, we were able to rebuild our relationship on new, beautiful ground. Two years later we married. And today our son is eighteen months old.

When I decided to live for God, I knew it had to be all the way. I didn't know at the time what the costs of that decision

drained

would be, and I'm still learning. Sibs is learning right along with me. My modelling career came to an end. I knew I couldn't stay in that lifestyle and be true to what I was feeling inside. So I quit and spent the next several years trying to find a vocation I could give myself to whole-heartedly.

One thing that's clear: life can't be lived selfishly. You've got to get out of your own little world and live for others. I spent so many years destroying my life and other people's through my own selfishness. I have to keep asking myself: What *is* there I can do? How can I help? I can't change the past, but I can spend the rest of my life trying to do something for others. I now work for a charity that tries to brighten the lives of children who have AIDS or are directly affected by it. Just being able to spend three or four hours a week with each of the five children I visit makes a difference in their lives and mine.

Joshua died not long ago, at the age of four. He was born with AIDS. I used to hold him in my arms, and we'd dance around his mum's living room to MTV. We laughed a lot together. One time, we were dancing to a Bob Marley song, and I had this flashback: it was closing time at a night-club in Milan, and there I was, surrounded by women, the star of the show as usual, drinking and dancing to that very same song. Worlds collide. Right then I understood that God does move mountains. These are the mountains. And moving them is a far greater miracle than moving any physical mountain.

Both Ashley and Sibs have certainly experienced dramatic changes in their lives through their search for peace and meaning. For them, change came as the result of choices they made. Choices face each of us continually. Some are easy to make, while others require careful consideration. Each involves an element of risk: there is always the question, 'What if…?' But in speaking with the men and women whose insights are included in this book, a common thread stands out: the role of choice and free will in their search for peace.

Holocaust survivor and prominent psychiatrist Viktor Frankl has written that peace means freedom in the face of three things: our instincts, our inherited traits and our surroundings.

> Certainly man has instincts, but these instincts must not have him. As for inheritance, research on heredity has shown how high is the degree of human freedom in the face of predisposition. As for environment, we know that it does not make man, but that everything depends on what man makes of it, on his attitude toward it.
>
> Thus, man is by no means merely a product of heredity and environment. There is another element: decision. Man ultimately decides for himself! And, in the end, education must be education toward the ability to decide.

Few of us, Frankl goes on, make important life choices with any degree of decisiveness. Backtracking here and compromising there, we often lack the backbone to stand by our own decisions. Because of this we remain in a continual state of angst. At times we hold a planless, day-to-day attitude toward whatever comes our way. At others we are fatalistic, defeatist. One day we exhibit spinelessness and have no clearly defined opinion at all; the next we cling so strongly and stubbornly to an idea we become fanatical. To quote Yeats, 'The best lack all conviction, while the worst / Are full of passionate intensity.' Ultimately, all these symptoms can be traced back to our fear of responsibility, and the indecision which it spawns.

I still remember clearly the day my pluck was first put to the test. As a fourteen-year-old in a New York school, I was required to recite the Pledge of Allegiance to the United States flag every day. As an immigrant, I found the practice bizarre, and the unquestioning nationalism it nurtured disturbed me. Each morning a different student took a turn leading it. The day my turn came, I got up in front of the class and told them that I would not do it. My ultimate allegiance belonged to God, I said, not to a piece of cloth.

You could have heard a pin drop, my teacher and classmates were so stunned. This was unthinkable! It was the height of the Cold War and the McCarthy era, when anyone stepping out of line was automatically suspected of being a communist informer and a traitor. In Washington, the infamous House Un-American Activities Committee hearings were in full swing. By the end of the morning, I had been reported to the principal and brought before a gathering of the entire faculty to explain myself. Shocked as they were, they showed understanding once I clarified my position and assured them I had meant no disrespect, but had acted only out of my conviction that doing the right thing was more important than doing the 'patriotic' thing.

At home, my parents were somewhat surprised, though supportive. To my father, it was simple: if you didn't follow your conscience, you would never find peace. If doing this meant rocking the boat, so be it. That was always preferable to sitting back and pretending everything was fine.

JOHN WINTER, a now-elderly Englishman whom I have known since my youth, wrote in a recent letter that the most productive chapters of his life were those he entered with a firm decision – and the intention of sticking to it, come what may.

I left school at sixteen and started working in the lab of a firm that made lead pipe and paint, and went up to London to study for a science degree in the evenings. When I was nineteen I had to register for military service. I was unwilling to sanction the horrors of war, so I had decided to register as a conscientious objector. When I told my boss, he pointed out that the firm was now making bullets instead of pipes and paint, and that my stand wouldn't quite go together with the company's. I was in shock, and can still remember that weekend as if it were today – the hours spent trying to discern what I should do. I couldn't honestly carry on with my job, but to leave it seemed unthinkable too.

A friend of mine was going through similar tensions at this time. However, finding no solid basis on which to stake his refusal to take part in the war, he later changed his mind and joined the Royal Air Force.

That weekend – when I had to choose whether I was going to be true to what I believed about war, and act on it, or go on with life as usual – was decisive for me. It cost me many sleepless hours, but finally I knew what I had to do: give up my job.

It seems a very small thing now, but it was very big for me then. Perhaps it was the first time I really had to choose between my own wishes and what my conscience was telling me to do. I can only say now, fifty-eight years later, that at that moment I experienced something of true, unwavering peace. I have had to think of it several times since then in my life, when my conscience has prodded me to take a step I didn't want to take at first. Each time I have followed my conscience, and it has led to inner peace.

On the other side of the coin, life has also made me realize that if you hear a call but don't follow, it does something to you inside, and maybe the next time you won't be able to hear the call as clearly – or it may never come again.

After I left my job I was unemployed for months and months. I looked for work that was not connected with the war, but there was none, at least not in what I was trained for. To be idle is a terrible thing. I couldn't even find work in an office or shop. Yet I cannot deny that even then I was at peace about what I had done.

All of us know people who (unlike John) cannot find peace within themselves because they cannot stick to a decision. They go through life like a sailboat without a keel, tipping at the slightest gusts and reaching the goals they set out to meet only with the greatest trouble. Some never make it at all, but spend year after year trying to decide what to throw themselves into next. In a few cases I know of, such paralyzing indecision has led to emotional imbalance and even complete mental instability.

Peace comes about through decisiveness. Life is filled with influences – some good, some bad – vying for our attention. If we are undecided about what course we want our life to take, we run the risk of being tugged in countless directions. Of course, decisiveness means little unless we are ready to embrace the changes and consequences it brings. This readiness extends to every aspect of our lives: readiness to forgive the unforgivable; to remember where we would sooner forget; to forget where we would rather remember. It means readiness to love where we have hated; to go where we would rather not go, and to wait if we have been forgotten; to look forward, not back; to draw a line under the past and turn in hope toward the future. Ultimately, it means readiness to give everything, even our own life.

9 Choose Life

Do not go gentle into that good night.
Rage, rage against the dying of the light.

DYLAN THOMAS

Beheaded by the Nazis in 1943 for her involvement with the White Rose, a Munich-based student group that wrote, printed and distributed anti-government leaflets, Sophie Scholl was no ordinary twenty-one-year-old. She was no ordinary activist either. In *The Resistance of the White Rose*, author Inge Scholl, her sister, remembers the strange peace that accompanied her, guiding her and giving her strength.

When Sophie first came across the White Rose and discovered that her brother Hans was its founder and most active participant, she was angry. At the same time she felt it was a lonely voice for truth and that unless she supported it, it might soon be drowned out by the growing clamour of propaganda and lies. So she threw all her energy into it.

Several years before, Hans and Sophie had both embraced Hitler's promises of a new Germany with enthusiasm. Yet after they began to realize how many consciences and lives were being trampled by the dictator's demonic lust for power, they grew increasingly determined to swim against the stream. By late 1942 it was hard to find a more vigorous cell of opposition, or a more endangered one.

In February 1943 the leaders of the White Rose were identified and captured, and within five days the Scholls and their closest supporters were dead. Further executions followed in April and July.

The Scholls went to their end bravely, even proudly. When Sophie heard her sentence – death by guillotine – she is said to have reacted calmly: 'Such a fine, sunny day, and I have to go. But what does it matter, if through us thousands of others are awakened and stirred to action?' Here was an inner peace born of unshakeable faith in the rightness of her cause.

Doubtless, Sophie went through moments of intense fear, but she refused to go back on her decision to fight with all her strength the evils of Hitler's Reich. Today, such conviction is a rare thing. (Which of us cares so deeply about our beliefs that we are willing to be killed for them?) So is the reassurance and peace it brings in the face of struggle. Unless we are fully convinced of the rightness of what we are doing, we will never be able to face a similar test with such stamina. Nor will we experience the satisfaction of knowing that our life, even if cut short, has counted for something.

Every day of our lives, we are faced with uncertainties, and these can easily give rise to fears within us. While each of us may battle our own particular set of fears, there is one fear that seems to pose the greatest challenge to human confidence and security: our universal fear of death.

If anyone had a reason to fear death, it was Martin Luther King. Immensely charismatic and unabashedly outspoken, he put his life on the line for the cause of racial equality time and again. In the end, of course, he paid the ultimate price. Like anyone else, King must have been afraid of dying, yet the few times I met him or heard him speak, he radiated a deep calm and peace. Here was a man with no doubts as to his mission, and no crippling fears about the cost of carrying it out. 'No man is free if he fears death,' he told the crowd at a civil rights rally in 1963. 'But the minute you conquer the fear of death, at that moment you are free.' Friends urged him to take fewer risks, but he shrugged them off. 'I cannot worry about my safety,' he told them. 'I cannot live in fear. I have to function. If there is one fear I have conquered, it is the fear of death.... I submit to you that if a man hasn't discovered something that he will die for, he isn't fit to live!'

IN THE 1994 MOVIE 'The Shawshank Redemption', Andy Dufresne (Tim Robbins) spends decades behind bars for two murders he did not commit. Though his situation seems hopeless, he does not succumb to despair. Instead, with only a small rock hammer to aid him, he sets about the painstaking process of tunnelling through the thick prison walls. For him, the issue is simple. As he explains to his friend Red (Morgan Freeman), there are only two choices in life: 'Get busy living, or get busy dying.' It's a choice none of us can escape.

When Carole and her husband, Dale, moved to our community in the mid-1970s, it was obvious from the start that she belonged in the 'get busy living' category. Her outspokenness and her ability to call a spade a spade rattled some people, but many (teenagers and young adults, in particular) found in her a warm-hearted and trustworthy friend. Though at times she battled bouts of severe depression and felt cut off from those around her, she never surrendered to her fears. For her, there was only one option: life.

In 1995, at the age of fifty-three, Carole was diagnosed with breast cancer. A first round of chemotherapy resulted in remission, but in March 1998 the cancer returned. Tests showed it had spread to both her lungs. That it would kill her seemed inevitable; specialists told her she could expect to die within months. By the beginning of summer, she was losing ground noticeably and required strong pain medication, though she insisted on going about her daily work as usual. Her daughter's wedding, planned for early July, was rescheduled and held in June; Carole was afraid she might otherwise miss it.

But Carole was a fighter, and she never seemed to stay on the ropes for long. Again and again, she amazed her husband and those of us who knew her – and herself too, most likely – bouncing back from the edge of death, just when we thought she was going. We should have known better: Carole planned to die on her feet, at the office where she worked. She seemed to know she was living on borrowed time, and she wasn't about to misspend any of it. There were too many things still to do, too many people in need of an encouraging word or a friendly smile: she simply didn't have *time* to die, she said.

Carole died on December 1, 1998. By rights, she should have been dead long before. But Carole never knew how to quit, and she had viewed her illness as just another challenge to tackle head-on. In a magazine interview five months before her death, she spoke of her struggle to live life to its fullest:

> When I first heard I had cancer, I was just terrified, because I have always been terribly afraid of death. But that only lasted a few minutes after I heard the diagnosis. In fact, I felt somehow relieved – I don't know why. Maybe it's because I had always been afraid of dying, and all of a sudden there it was – cancer – and I didn't have to worry about it anymore.

Sure, I've gone to pieces over it since then. After the first bout of chemotherapy, I was sitting there and I felt this lump under my arm, and I just fell apart. I guess I still hadn't really faced the possibility of terminal cancer, not at that point anyway.

This is going to sound really dumb, but it's the truth: I've been almost frantically afraid of cancer all my life, but then when it came, right there, square in my face, I wasn't afraid anymore. I don't like to use the word 'gift' because it's overused, but that really was a gift. Dale and I looked at each other, and we said, 'Here it is. Now we're in God's hands.'

Dale even joked about it when we found out that I had cancer; he said it would be a terrible shame if I died of something else, since I had worried so much about cancer all my life.

Obviously, you don't just lie down once you know you've got cancer. You don't just fold up and crash. You fight to keep living with everything you have. That's why I thought chemotherapy was the answer at first, because I felt I was really fighting the disease with everything I had. I was going to take the most explosive kind, you know – whatever it took.

Then I found out it was a hopeless cancer; that people just didn't survive it. I think they told me the survival rate was basically nil, 1 to 99. But I hadn't asked, and I didn't care. I already knew from my sister who died of the same cancer that the statistics were pretty bleak. That's when I said, 'Forget the numbers. I'm not going to spend the rest of my life in bed, sick and vomiting and everything else. I'm going to *live* with everything I've got.'

Living with cancer, you begin to realize that you have to make use of every day; each minute becomes precious. You know, we spend a lot of our time dealing with petty problems and thinking petty thoughts, and I've come to see that that's a complete drain and has to go. There's anger, envy, every kind of emotion you have in a relationship with anybody. People hurt each other, and get hurt over little things. I've come to see that it's stupid –just plain stupid – to waste time on those things. Dale and I have talked about how we've probably wasted years of our lives carrying little grudges and things that we couldn't work out, or struggling to find enough humility to confront a problem, or apologize, or whatever.

The present moment – the time we have right now – is the same for you as it is for me or for anyone. It's all we have. We tend to think, 'I'll do that tomorrow;' or, 'I'll wait till I have time to follow through on that…' But we actually don't have tomorrow. None of us does. We only have today and we only have each other – the person next to us, the person we live with or work with. Seeing this has been a tremendous challenge to me. I can remember yesterday, but I can't re-live yesterday, and I have no idea what tomorrow will bring. All I have is just right now.

Yesterday I didn't think I was going to live another day, and the doctors and my family didn't think so either. Today I don't feel that close to death. But that's what is so exciting, because it forces you to live in the right-now, in the present. It might seem crazy that I'm still coming here to the office every morning, but you have no idea how much it means to me. At work I run into all the people I love. I don't want to be at home staring at four walls – I want to be around people, joking and laughing and sometimes crying too. I definitely couldn't stand being alone in bed.

It's wonderful to be able to live just as if you're going to keep going. I guess that's the advice I'd give anybody: to go on as long as you can, in whatever way you can.

Each of us has a life to live – and once we've found it, we ought to live for it. We need to be ready to give up everything – our plans, absolutely everything, in order to go after what we've found. I'm not saying we all have to be intense or energetic. It's not a personality thing. But to really *live* demands all our fire.

10 Say Thank-you

Live your life so that the fear of death can never enter your heart. When you arise in the morning, give thanks for the morning light. Give thanks for your life and strength. Give thanks for your food and for the joy of living. And if perchance you see no reason for giving thanks, rest assured the fault is in yourself.

ASCRIBED TO CHIEF TECUMSEH

Most of us have no difficulty saying 'thank-you' when good things come our way. But to give thanks from the bottom of our hearts for what ever each day brings, even if it's bad, is work for a lifetime. The medieval mystic Meister Eckhart once suggested that if the only prayer we ever said was 'thank-you', it would still suffice. If we take his advice superficially, it might be easy enough to follow. Yet what does true thankfulness really mean? Writer Henri Nouwen, who left the limelight of his Yale University professorship to live and work in a communal home for the mentally disabled, once wrote:

> To be grateful for the good things that happen in our lives is easy, but to be grateful for all of our lives – the good as well as the bad, the moments of joy as well as the moments of sorrow, the successes as well as the failures, the rewards as well as the rejections – that requires hard spiritual work. Still, we are only truly grateful people when we can say thank-you to all that has brought us to the present moment.

Because there is so much in life we cannot control, we must learn to look at things that test us not as obstacles, but as opportunities for growth. So long as we shrink from every predicament, every situation that frightens us or sets us on edge, we will never know peace. This does not mean we must silently accept everything that comes our way. Yet often it is just when struggles or problems weigh most heavily on us that gratitude can change our entire outlook on life. As someone told me recently: 'Once when I was in a deep depression, it occurred to me that if I looked for even just one thing to be thankful for, that would be the first step up. There is always something you can find to be happy about.'

On the eve of his execution, Dietrich Bonhoeffer wrote to his fiancée, Maria Wedemeyer: 'You must not think that I am unhappy. What is happiness and unhappiness? It depends so little on the circumstances; it depends really only on what happens inside a person. I am grateful every day that I have you, and that makes me happy.'

In my experience, the most common root of ingratitude is not hardship, but a false understanding of happiness. Bonhoeffer understood that the presence or absence of hardship need not have anything to do with our state of mind or soul. Most of us, though, attempt to weigh our happiness on an external scale –good things stacked against bad. As for the good things – family, food, house, friends, love, work – if we are honest, we must admit that we often take them for granted. We treat them as rights, rather than gifts.

Nothing can satisfy us when selfish expectations make us discontented with our lot; hence the cliché, 'The grass is always greener on the other side of the fence.' So long as our vision is limited by the blinkers of our own wants and needs, we will not be able to see those of others, let alone the things we have to be

Free Book offer

- To give to colleagues, friends or relatives
- Request larger quantities for free* distribution at events.
- Display for people to pick up at work, school or church.

Please send me books as marked to the right:

Name _____

Organisation _____

Address _____

Address _____

City _____ Post Code _____

Email or Telephone number (mandatory) _____

Plough

Or request your books on

Email: contact@ploughbooks.co.uk

Free phone: 0800 018 0799

Rich in Years
Finding peace and purpose in a long life. Rediscover the spiritual riches that age has to offer.

[Qty]

Escape Routes
Maps the way out of loneliness, frustration, alienation and despair through real-life stories.

[Qty]

Why Children Matter
Offers concrete steps to encourage parents who want to pass on to their children the values their parents gave them.

[Qty]

Their Name is Today
Addresses current issues that threaten childhood and suggests creative ways to help children, families and teachers.

[Qty]

Why Forgive?
Stories of people who overcame scars left by violent crime, interpersonal strife and their own failures.

[Qty]

Yes, please send me a FREE trial copy of the **Plough Quarterly**. A bold, hope-filled magazine to inspire faith and action. 72pp full colour

[Yes]

View our full list of titles at **www.plough.com**

*Donations are appreciated. Cheques payable to Plough Publishing

Freepost Plus RTHT-UBYG-KTXK
Plough Publishing House
Darvell
Brightling Road
ROBERTSBRIDGE
TN32 5DR

grateful for. My father once wrote to an unhappy friend, 'You will always find reasons to grumble. If you want to find peace, you must be willing to give them up.'

On the theme of gratefulness in the face of catastrophe, the Old Testament story of Job stands second to none. Discussed by generations of readers (as much for the beauty of its verses as for its content), it is the account of a man who has everything – productive lands, flourishing herds, industrious servants and a loving family – but loses it all in a flash. To compound his suffering further, boils break out all over his body, and his friends accuse him of having brought his own suffering – and his children's deaths – upon himself by doing something utterly heinous...though they can't say what, and have to spend the rest of the book guessing. Even Job's wife turns against him, urging him to 'curse God and die'. Yet despite his devastation, he refuses to let bitterness ruin him. Against all reason (his own included), Job clings doggedly to faith in the God who, he believes, granted him life in the first place.

WILLIAM MARVIN is a priest in Alabama I first had contact with when he offered to help our community send humanitarian aid to Cuba. William has had more than his fair share (if there is such a thing) of suffering, but I have never heard him complain. Despite one Job-like test after the next – a near-fatal illness, the death of his youngest son, the loss of his job and a divorce – he is still able to recognize that others have endured even greater suffering. It is this attitude, I suspect, that is the key to his sense of peace.

My mother died suddenly when I was eight years old. A little over a year later my father married a woman much younger than he. Ours was not a happy home. My father was a school

administrator, noted for strict enforcement of discipline and high academic standards. He carried this into the home. I wasn't mistreated physically, though my stepmother did slap me a time or two. Sarcasm and derision were the weapons of choice. The standing rule was, 'What "Mother" says, goes!' My teenage rebellion took the form of doing just enough in school to pass. This was the one area where I could defy them both, because it was so important to them. As soon as I graduated from high school
I was told to leave. I lived with an uncle and aunt until I was old enough to be drafted into the army. My years in the service were intense. I saw battles, and saw men die. I was injured. After the army I went to college, though I had no clear sense of what to do with my life.

I married and soon had two sons, a house in the suburbs, a mortgage and a car, and I worked as a postman. Three or four years later I became very discontented. Through much soul-searching and advice-seeking, I decided to become an Episcopal priest. After two months in seminary we went on a retreat. I was overwhelmed. I went to the retreat master, a monk from the Order of the Holy Cross, and told him that I had made a mistake: I was not worthy. His response was, 'Of course you're not! None of us are. But we are what God has to work with.'

After his graduation and ordination, William served in several parishes but soon realized that his understanding of his position was different to that of his superiors. Before long he was relieved of his duties. He found no new openings for a long time; after all, he had spoken out strongly against the direction the Episcopal Church was taking. Finally he found a place in the parish where he now serves.

During those years, tragedy struck repeatedly. William's youngest son was killed in a traffic accident; then his wife became involved with another man and moved out of the house, after which they divorced; his second son succumbed to alcohol and died at thirty-five of a massive stroke. There were some satisfactions, it is true: his eldest son became a successful lawyer; his daughter earned a Ph.D. and joined the faculty of prestigious Notre Dame University. William himself has found a family among the warm-hearted members of his parish. Yet his life has been anything but easy.

Have I found peace? I think so. I've fulfilled my obligations to my children; I am caring for the people of this parish, and I plan to do so as long as God wills.

I have yet one thing I must do. I must die. Until then, even though I do plan ahead, I try to live each day as if it is my last.

It is not too much to believe that I have been in the hand of God from the day of my birth. My sons did not die, nor did my wife abandon her wedding vows, so that I would be tempered. These things happened because it is an imperfect world. Twenty-one years ago – after I had been fired from the church, my youngest son had been killed, my wife was recovering from a heart attack (and about to leave me), and I was working only ten hours a week – a friend suggested that I must feel as did Job. I said, 'Well, I've not suffered boils.' And I've *still* not suffered boils.

Today I went, as I do every Friday, to the bedside of a man, a retired physician. He is dying. He has lost three daughters to cancer. His wife had cancer surgery a few years ago. Sundays I take Communion to him. He is not the only parishioner to have been given the special grace to bear burdens. Nearly everyone has at one time or another been visited by travail. One young mother suffered third-degree burns over forty percent of her body. Her husband abandoned her, and she is raising three young children alone. She is doing it very well. That God has permitted me to know people such as these, and to share my life with them, has been a great reward. I am grateful. It has brought me peace.

say thank-you

ıı That Gnawing Feeling

The object of life is not to be on the side
of the majority, but to escape finding oneself
in the ranks of the insane.

MARCUS AURELIUS

No matter how unique each person's search for peace may appear, a common thread ties them together. To a greater or lesser extent, everyone is on a journey toward wholeness. Some people say they are seeking peace of mind; others, peace of heart. Some are searching for fellowship, and others for community. Some are looking for inner serenity; others, global harmony. Underneath, all of these quests are motivated by a sense of the fragmentation of life, and by the desire for it to be overcome.

Life is full of divisions: between the home and the workplace; the private and the public; the job and the leisure-time activity; the political, the professional and the personal. In itself, there is nothing wrong with this. The problems begin when these separate realms create contradictions and conflicts. Before long, inconsistency can become compromise, and after that, even hypocrisy.

My friend Charles Headland once told me it was the compartmentalization of his life that set him searching for peace. As an accountant with a large Croydon firm, he had one set of friends; as a peace activist, another; as a church member, still another; and finally, his family. Nothing connected these sectors, and each day had to be balanced so as to fulfil his commitments to all four.

Back in the 1960s, Daniel Berrigan, a Jesuit priest, made national headlines when he and eight others (his brother Philip was among them) raided the draft board office in Catonsville, Maryland, and dragged all the draft files they could get their hands on out into the street. Then, in front of a small audience of newspaper and television reporters, they poured home-made napalm over the files and set them ablaze – an act of protest against the Vietnam War. It was not only the war's fundamental injustice, Berrigan says, that prompted him to take such a dramatic step, but also the 'fragmented conscience' that lay at the root of the compromise and hypocrisy of so many priests and ministers. In peacetime, they would preach enthusiastically on the Ten Commandments, especially 'thou shalt not kill'. But in wartime, these same clergymen were only too willing to bless bombers, which were used to drop napalm not merely on enemy targets but also on innocent villagers.

In the years since the Vietnam War ended, Berrigan's unflinching commitment to peace has won him countless admirers and friends, as well as his share of enemies. But the same inconsistency has shown itself again and again: anti-war people are pro-abortion, and militarists are pro-life; anti-abortion activists are pro-death penalty, and so on. 'Everyone wants to get rid of some particular evil, after which they feel the world is going to be a better place,' he concludes. 'They forget that you can't be for the bomb and for children at the same time.'

Rabbi Kenneth L. Cohen has said much the same. In a recent essay he reminds readers of the horrifying two-facedness of

Nazi life, where friendly husbands and fathers 'shot Jews in the morning and listened to Mozart in the afternoon'. The example is extreme, but it highlights the potential end of every path where conflicts run unresolved and threaten not only peace, but life itself.

Charles Moore, a former college instructor, longed for wholeness in his life but could not find it. Eventually he concluded that as long as *he* was at the centre of his personal search he would never find a satisfactory answer.

When I reflect on my life even ten years ago, I see that I was living a slow death of gradual disintegration. The explosive energy of my youth was fast becoming dissipated, not because of reckless living, but as a result of obsessively attempting to hold everything together. It was a meltdown of my own choosing. I was obsessed with trying hard, being good, meeting needs and doing the right thing. There were so many good causes to join, so much knowledge to master, so many people to meet, so many relationships to build, so many obligations to fulfil and so many opportunities to explore. I wanted everything, and I got what I wanted. But there was no existential coherence. I was fragmented inside and out.

How all this happened is easier for me to see now than it was then. I was simply unable to integrate the disparate, dangling threads of an over-full life. Individually and singly, the threads could not be joined together into a meaningful whole.

There was my work as a professor, and my own graduate studies. Both demanded my time; both demanded my allegiance. Joined together only in 'idea', these two parts of my life were in fact worlds apart. Then there were professional relationships with colleagues to maintain, though apart from our shared academic interests, we had little in common.

As life's demands increased, my strength did not. Besides, I had other concerns, other interests. There was my personal life –

my wife Leslie, my friends and hers, my family and hers – with multifarious dimensions that never quite seemed to intersect. Sometimes they overlapped, but they never really came together. Try as I might, I couldn't 'get it together'. Unable to let any one thing go, yet overwhelmed by keeping everything simultaneously under control, I created elaborate coping mechanisms which I perceived would get me through. I had a confidential counselling relationship with a close friend; I made opportunities for 'release' through leisure, entertainment, etc., with my wife; I learned to reschedule my graduate studies and readjust my teaching load; I backed out of this or that time-consuming relationship, and so forth. But paring down, adjustment and mending never did the trick. Well-intentioned and dedicated as I was, I was frantic and frayed, and my life remained disconnected.

Now that I look back, it seems ironic how full, yet how incomplete, my life felt. I had virtually everything I ever wanted: meaningful employment, intellectual excitement, altruistic outlets, caring friends, material success and freedom to adjust my schedule whenever I felt the need to do so. But I was not at peace. The boundaries of my life were wide, and I kept all my options open.

In retrospect I see I was playing right into that grand deception: it's *your* life; do with it what you want. I had made my life the centre of the universe, even under the guise of serving others. Despite my efforts to live selflessly, I was trapped in the madness of a middle-class lifestyle that revolved – not only ultimately, but in the most mundane ways – around *my* wants and desires. I just couldn't see that this kind of living was unreal, untrue.

No matter how many ways I tried to compensate for the lack of synthesis in my life, it wasn't until I stopped living on terms centred on personal fulfilment and independence that I began to find some sense of coherence. And I saw that I had a choice to make: I could continue living in that way, negotiating a multi-

drained

plicity of demands and relationships of my own choosing; or I could begin anew on an altogether different foundation, one where community (not self) and mutual service (not personal fulfilment) were the premise.

I don't think the question of personal peace will ever go away entirely. But the intent of my heart and the course of my actions are no longer at odds: the inner and outer dimensions of my life actually cohere; and they are held together, not strenuously, by force of will, but by a deep sense of peace. And the mystery of it is that it came into my life not because I struggled for it, but because my eyes were opened to see past the myth of self-fulfilment, and into the reality of a more abundant life.

FOR MARK AND PAULINE, the search for wholeness and peace began long before they met and married in Belfast. Born to working-class parents, Mark spent the first ten years of his life in a tightly-knit mining village, just outside Birmingham, where a sense of community pervaded, despite life's hardships. Then his family moved to a council housing estate in a larger, industrial town, and the happiness of his childhood years slowly ebbed. When he was fifteen, his parents divorced. Feeling hurt and betrayed, Mark had a hard time trusting anyone. He left school without sitting his exams and stayed with his mother, but tensions mounted, and at seventeen he left home.

Not knowing in which direction to head, Mark made his way to London, hoping to find work and a sense of purpose.

> I was always looking for something real and genuine. I looked at a lot of different religions, groups and movements, but I saw too much hypocrisy. I was determined not to be a part of something which to me didn't seem to be the truth. That's what motivated me: the search for truth. At that time, I guess I would have defined truth as something unselfish. If I saw a selfish reason for

something, it didn't seem to me to be true. But at the same time, though I didn't realize it then, I myself was extremely selfish.

Ten years of restless seeking led Mark to Northern Ireland – via factory jobs and homelessness in London, long periods of solitude, spates of drug abuse, time behind bars, and overland trips to a Tibetan Buddhist monastery and an Indian ashram.

In Belfast, he was introduced to Pauline by a mutual friend. She was studying art at Ulster Polytechnic. The two couldn't have come from more diverse backgrounds. Pauline had been born in England, but at the age of four she and her parents had moved to Northern Ireland; her father worked in management for a large firm and was transferred there. She remembers:

I had a protected childhood, in many ways. Being a well-off English family, we were able to live in a nice place ten miles outside Belfast. I attended a Protestant school, and Irish history was simply not taught. But our family wasn't really part of the Northern Ireland Protestant culture. We weren't churchgoers. My father sympathized with the Catholics, who were treated as second-class citizens at the factory where he worked.

I remember when the Troubles started, and suddenly we weren't allowed to go into Belfast anymore, and we started seeing the British Army all over the place. Still, it wasn't until I became a teenager and started to get to know people up in Belfast that I realized just how much it was destroying their lives. But it took years until I really understood what was going on. Because somebody from my background just didn't see it, unless you went looking for it.

Rebelling against her privileged upbringing, Pauline left Northern Ireland at seventeen, spending a year at art school in the north of England before returning home and taking up her studies at Ulster Polytechnic.

The one thing I knew I didn't want was a conventional life – a nice house, a nice car, a nice job and so on. That was where my peers were heading; it was what they wanted. I felt I had to get away.

Later, Pauline headed back to England to continue her studies at Portsmouth:

Art school was all about self-expression; there was no guidance at all. We were just supposed to go in and express ourselves from dawn till dusk! It was at the height of the punk-rock era, and people were expressing very violent feelings. Deep down, there was a hunger among us young people for love and for truth, but because of an overriding sense of hopelessness, it was often expressed in a dark and self-destructive way. The prevailing mood was a very damaging one. We students lived in squats, and some were sleeping around and smoking dope. The feeling of emptiness – you just couldn't live with it; it destroyed you.

Having thrown out almost all moral values, I had nothing left to hold on to, and I hurt many people very badly, including myself. I knew my life was falling to pieces, and I started to search for some meaning to it. I tried going to a few churches in Portsmouth. I didn't go to any services, but I just walked in and spent some time alone. Just doing that lost me a friend. By the end of a year, I was on the verge of a complete break-down, and I headed back to Northern Ireland, happy to return to a friendlier, more caring environment.

I got a job as a cook at the hostel for paroled young people where Mark was already working. Our seeking drove us together; it wasn't like we'd fallen head over heels in love at first sight or anything like that. But we both knew we could go on and on seeking together, and neither of us was going to say, 'Okay, this is where we stop. We've gone far enough.'

Eventually Pauline and Mark married, left the inner-city and, with some inherited money, purchased a cottage in Donegal. The secluded quiet brought space for reflection, and for a while they were content to feed off the natural beauty of their surroundings. But before long a nagging sense of loneliness set in. After their daughter was born, they moved back to England, where their search continued. Mark goes on:

> We'd tried different churches, different religions. I didn't read the Bible very much, but what I did read made me feel that there was something real and genuine in the life of Jesus. I didn't really know how it applied to my own life, and I didn't see that same genuineness in the churches I'd been to before – it all seemed a bit soppy.
>
> We lived near London for a while and joined a church where we felt the members took their beliefs seriously. But before long it became clear that here, too, was a lot of unhappiness and disunity. People harboured grudges and talked behind other people's backs, and we couldn't accept that.

Moving down to Bristol, Pauline and Mark joined a handful of friends living together in two adjacent houses, in the middle of St. Paul's, the city's worst neighbourhood. Prostitutes stood at street corners, drugs were sold in broad daylight and murders were not infrequent. Here they tried to create an atmosphere of community. As Mark puts it, 'We were sort of punk Christians, and living and sharing together wasn't easy. But we felt that we were taking steps closer to the life of truth we were seeking.'

Within a year the group disintegrated, and Mark and Pauline decided to look around further. 'We were searching for something radically different from anything we'd ever known,' Mark recounts. 'To us, it was clear that we had to live together with others if we were ever going to feel whole as individuals.'

Their travelling and searching finally paid off. Together, they discovered a community where people worked hard to build genuine, frank relationships and eliminate gossip. As Mark puts it, 'It was a place where people stuck together, through thick and thin, and helped each other when things weren't going well. It was a place where I could learn to trust others once again.'

Fourteen years later, they are still there. But neither of them would claim to have 'arrived' at a state of constant peace. Like the rest of us, their search goes on with each new day. 'We find wholeness and peace,' Pauline says, 'by turning away from the things that we've done wrong in the past.'

At first, the harm our own selfishness had done to others – through uncommitted sexual relationships, for example – was extremely painful to face. But recognizing our need to change, and putting right what wrongs we could, brought us new freedom and gave us courage to move on. We still make plenty of mistakes, and sometimes we hurt each other or those around us. But we can always say we're sorry and put things right, and then go forward again. This softens our hearts and makes our love for those around us grow stronger. It's what keeps us alive.

12 Forget Yourself

Don't let difficulties depress or divert you;
don't be so worried about yourself.
The cause that should grip each one of us
is so great that our small weaknesses
can't destroy it.

EBERHARD ARNOLD

We will never arrive at a perfect state of peace,
or find it once and for all. We can follow the
stepping stones across the water as cautiously
and earnestly as we like, but on the other
side we will still be ourselves. All the same, there is no question
that once we experience peace, our hearts are opened to a new
dimension of living.

Several of the people who contributed to this book told me
that the peace they are looking for, and the peace they want to
share with others, is best described as a fullness of life. To them,
seeking peace as an end in itself is too self-serving an exercise:
'Now I've found peace. What next?' The life they are looking for
does not necessarily preclude tears and hardships, yet its fullness comes to expression in freedom and joy, compassion and
justice.

Josef Ben-Eliezer, a European of Jewish descent, spent much
of his youth in search of such a life, though as a young man he
would not have described it that way:

What motivated my searching was the hatred and bloodshed I saw in my childhood and youth, especially during World War II, when my family fled from Germany to Poland, then to Siberia, and finally to Israel. I felt peace could be found only in the context of an answer to the universal need for brotherhood, and that is what drove me to seek it.

I was involved in the national liberation movement in Israel, and the conflicts that it entailed, but turned away from it after I realized that, having come to power, this movement had become an oppressive one. So instead I looked for an answer in world revolution. I studied Marx, Lenin and Trotsky. Later, in Paris, I became involved in various leftist causes. But a nagging question occupied me more and more: where is the guarantee that if the revolution is victorious, those who gain power will not end up oppressing the masses themselves, as happened in Russia and elsewhere?

Then I began reading about the very first Christians, and something completely new struck me. I saw that the church in the first few centuries of its existence was a truly revolutionary movement, proclaiming a new order and living it. The Jesus these people followed was not the Jesus of conventional Christianity, but the real, historical Son of God, who overcomes division between person and person, nation and nation.

In time, my years of searching for an answer to the forces that drive people apart led me into contact with other like-minded individuals. I believe every person longs for unity of heart with others. But there needs to be a change of heart before it can be accepted. That is why it is necessary to turn around, to flip our lives upside down. I experienced that as well, and continue to experience it.

Few of us experience such oneness with those around us. We are resigned to disunity and anxiety; it's 'just the way things are'. More often than not the distractions of day-to-day life,

drained

as well as our own stupidity and dullness, keep us from seeing farther than the ends of our noses. If we do seek peace, we tend to go after it selfishly.

Writing of the search for peace in his own life, Thomas Merton, an American monk who understood the value of both contemplation and social action, suggested that it must go hand in hand with what he called the 'openness of love'.

> The contemplative life is the search for peace…not in a barren, negative closing of the senses upon the world, but in the openness of love.
>
> When I came to this monastery where I am, I came in revolt against the meaningless confusion of a life in which there was so much activity, so much movement, so much useless talk, so much superficial and needless stimulation, that I could not remember who I was. But the fact remains that my flight from the world is not a reproach to you who remain in the world, and I have no right to repudiate the world in a purely negative fashion, because if I do that my flight will have taken me not to truth and to God but to a private, though doubtless pious, illusion….

Before his death in 1968, Merton was involved in the early stages of setting up a new form of contemplative community in Central America – one that confronted injustice and stood up for the oppressed, while remaining firmly grounded in its commitment to love.

IN THE 1960s, David Brandon's work in radio and television – particularly his role in the acclaimed TV drama 'Cathy Come Home' – won him recognition across Britain. Today he is a professor at Anglia Polytechnic University, in Cambridge, teaching courses on community care. A committed Buddhist, David sets aside time each day for meditation, or 'sitting', as he terms it. On the surface, nothing hints at his history: his battered childhood and turbulent youth, or his attempts at suicide. But in talking with David, it becomes clear that the peace he now enjoys and tries to pass on to others has come at a price.

I was brought up in the poverty-stricken mining town of Sunderland, in the Northeast of England, not far from the Scottish border. My father was a very violent man, with a very short fuse; my first memories are of being beaten up. Sometimes my brother and I were locked in the coal shed; often we'd be kicked and punched, or sometimes my father would hit us with old tennis rackets and canes and things. Even when I was asleep in bed, my father would attack me. It was an atmosphere of brutality for us boys, and for our mother as well. She was quite frequently beaten up, sometimes very severely, and there would be blood and handfuls of pulled-out hair all over the floor.

As soon as I could, I ran away from home. By the time I was twelve, I was working twenty-five or thirty hours a week. I suppose you could say I had to grow up very early. I lived on the streets of London, sleeping out on the streets on piles of papers. Sometimes I stayed in Salvation Army hostels, which were often very violent, dangerous places to live.

David chose education as his escape route and became 'an examination-passing machine', churning his way through school and university, where he met his future wife, Althea. They married after graduation, and David began a career as a senior social worker, working with people with learning disabilities. Television and radio jobs soon followed, bringing fame and recognition with them. Two children were born, and life seemed comfortable enough. But peace was the last thing David was feeling.

drained

I recognized so much hypocrisy in the world – people's words and actions didn't match up – and I desperately wanted meaning in life. I started to go to different churches, trying to find something. I'm not sure exactly what I was looking for, but I know I didn't find it. I felt very lonely, very isolated.

By the time I reached my late twenties, my life came to a head. I went to the London School of Economics, to study social work. Money was non-existent, and we had to sell up and move in with my parents-in-law. Althea and I weren't getting along very well, and she was suffering from depression. At the same time, my grandmother was dying, my grandfather was sick, my mother was dying, my father was developing arteriosclerosis – every relative I could think of was close to the grave in one way or another.

The pressure was more than I could handle. I wound up completely drained and demoralized, and I found myself heading for suicide. I knew my situation was desperate, so I decided to do something about it, even though I didn't have the energy and was depressed as hell. I trained as a psychotherapist and ran a hostel for homeless women, right in the centre of Soho.

I'd written a book and at the event for its launching I ran into a Zen master. Without really knowing why, I asked her, 'Can I come and study with you?' She agreed. So then I began getting up at quarter to six and meditating for ninety minutes every morning. A lot of mornings I would feel like killing myself, but I would get up anyway. I needed discipline, and Zen provided that; with a fixed routine, I just didn't have time to kill myself! But my troubles were far from over.

I was making a TV series about violence when my father died. The producers persuaded me to do a programme about my own life, something I would never have done while my father was alive. The emotional cost was enormous, and for two or three months after doing this programme I was so depressed I could hardly move.

For some reason I decided to climb Helvellyn, one of the highest peaks in the Lake District. I had climbed a lot of mountains but not this one, and I had no idea why I felt like climbing it on that particular February day. But I set out.

I made it to Striding Edge, a ridge less than three feet wide – and I have serious vertigo… I'm out in the middle of a blizzard, knee-deep in snow. I can't see where I'm going, and there's a thousand-foot drop to the left and to the right. Then the next thing I know, I'm hanging onto a bush, realizing there's nothing but air below me, and a voice inside of me says, 'You came to kill yourself, David. This is it, just let go of this bush and you'll slide away, and you won't be a bother to anybody anymore.' At the same time another part of me thinks, how did you get into this position? This is ridiculous, let's get out of this!

Fortunately the bush had strong roots, and I managed to get back onto the path… I'm lying face down. I don't know how far it is forward, I don't know how far it is back. But the greatest feeling wells up within me: I desperately want to live. I want to live!

That was the turning point. I mean, I still get depressed every now and again, but ever since that day I'm determined to live and to live with ever-increasing vigour.

Through Zen, I've realized in a way that I had never understood before that I'm actually part of the world. It took time, but slowly I began to notice nature, to notice all the things that are now a constant source of joy to me. It was a big discovery, in a way, to realize that I am part of the world, that the world is part of me, and that the planet is inhabited. And then this made me aware that I had some kind of commitment to others. Because of my past – my childhood, my homelessness, etc – it was easy for me to be concerned with violence in other families, and to work so that other people wouldn't have to go through what I experienced.

I suppose I see myself now as a wounded healer; I can use my experiences of despair, of difficulty, of struggle as a means to reach others. I don't mean that I'm trying to prevent suffering, but I am trying to help people learn the meaning of their suffering.

The common approach is, metaphorically speaking, to go out onto the sidewalk and to pick up all the banana skins, so that no one slips. Me, I go down early in the morning and drop *more* banana skins. People say, 'Well, why would you be doing that?' And I tell them, 'Teaching is not about trying to prevent people from falling down, it's about trying to get them to use their eyes.' If you take the banana skins away, you're saying that life is banana-skin free. Well, it is not. Life is full of banana skins.

I try to teach people to use their eyes, to look where they're stepping. It's my responsibility to respect people, to help them learn the lessons life teaches. When you slip on a banana skin and fall down, discuss what happened and learn from it. I think that it is actually unwise to get in between people and what life is trying to teach them, but we all have a responsibility for each other.

David's thoughts take us far beyond the quest for mere peace of mind. His search for inner peace led him into encounters with others, and taught him that personal and interpersonal aspects of peace are inextricably interwoven. It is an age-old discovery, but one that each of us must make: that those who spend their lives working to lighten the burdens of others are most likely to find the peace they themselves are looking for.

13 The Golden Rule

This is the true joy of life: being used up for a purpose
recognized by yourself as a mighty one; being a force of
nature instead of a feverish, selfish little clod of ailments
and grievances, complaining that the world will not
devote itself to making you happy. I am of the opinion
that my life belongs to others, and as long as I live, it is
my privilege to do for them whatever I can.

GEORGE BERNARD SHAW

Of all the root causes for people feeling drained,
the most widespread is probably selfishness,
whether within themselves, in their relationships with others or in the world at large. It may
also be the hardest to weed out. Problems such as arrogance,
mistrust, anger or resentment can be addressed in a fairly
straightforward fashion; we can usually take specific steps to
uncover their cause and to overcome them. But selfishness is
often simply there – unnamed, unnoticed, yet so powerful and
deep-seated that it shapes our entire outlook on life.

Sometimes selfishness leads to obvious wrongdoing, such as
adultery, theft or fraud. At other times, as in the case of an egocentric search for personal happiness or holiness, it may take
such a 'harmless' form that we are unaware of its danger. Once
selfishness is recognized for what it is, however, there is a simple and universal antidote for it: service to others.

Service, in the words of sixteenth-century mystic Teresa of
Avila, is the act of being God to each other: 'God has no hands,

nor has he feet nor voice except ours; and through these he works.' Growing up in a large family on a farm where everyone had to work hard, I never heard anyone talk about service in this way, but looking back I am sure my parents must have viewed it with similar respect.

Certainly we were taught its importance. When the only job my father could find was gardening in a leper colony, he made nothing of it. It could have meant contracting the disease and ending up there permanently, but he never told us children that. He said only that there was honour in doing the humblest service for others, and doing it gladly.

As for my mother, she was always active, bringing an elderly neighbour or a new mother a bouquet of flowers or a jar of preserves; missing a meal to sit with someone who was sick; getting up early to write to a lonely person or to finish knitting a gift.

Ruth Land, a retired doctor who worked for years on end in a rural South American clinic, says it is this sort of modest service that brings her the greatest satisfaction:

> You can look everywhere for peace, but you may not find it. Or you can forget yourself and get on with whatever work is there in front of you. That's what brings peace – doing whatever needs to be done in the house, showing love to your spouse, or whatever else comes to mind. If you do it for the sake of someone else, it will bring you peace.

An Indian story retold by Gandhi touches on a similar truth: the little acts of kindness we show to others are just as important as our nobler achievements. A troubled woman came to her guru, saying, 'O master, I find that I cannot serve God.' He asked, 'Is there nothing, then, that you love?' She responded,

'My little nephew.' And he said to her, 'There is your service to God, in your love for that child.'

Sometimes the greatest service is the one least noticed. In my community many elderly members work several hours a day, folding clothes in our laundry, classifying books in our library or helping in our wood and metal shops. In every case, the service they perform is invaluable, and not only in terms of what is produced. The sense of well-being and peace it gives them, and the joy that shines in their eyes when they speak about it, enriches our common life in a wonderful way. Their peace is infectious, spreading through the whole community.

Joe Bush, a seventy-five-year-old native of Ely who suffers from Parkinson's disease, was once a capable gardener. Now his activity is limited to sitting at a desk for a few hours each day, where he slowly progresses on a long translation project, one painstaking keystroke after another. Others might be frustrated, but not Joe: 'My work is pure joy.' Audrey, his wife, finds the same joy and peace through doing what she can for others:

> When Joe or I say, 'No thank-you, I can manage,' to those who care for us – half blind and lame as we are – it is not that we are ungrateful. It is just that life is more exciting if we can be useful for as long as we can. A tall candle does not suddenly go out when there is only an inch left; it burns on until there is just a little puddle of wax to show where it has been. There is still lots for us to do. Even when we are no longer able to do anything useful at all, we can still take comfort in that last line from Milton's sonnet 'On His Blindness', which he wrote at the end of his life after he had lost his sight: 'They also serve, who only stand and wait.'

Both Joe and Audrey say that their tasks are meaningful because they serve a purpose. A job is never just a job, if it does this. Without a purpose, work can be as meaningless, and create as much frustration and despair, as unemployment or enforced inactivity. According to Victor Frankl, the same is true of life in general:

> I have repeatedly seen that an appeal to continue life, to survive the most unfavourable conditions, can be made only when such survival appears to have a meaning. That meaning must be specific and personal, a meaning which can be realized by this one person alone and bring him peace of mind. For we must never forget that every person is unique in the universe.
>
> I remember my dilemma in a concentration camp when faced with a man and a woman who were close to suicide. Both had told me that they expected nothing more from life. I asked both my fellow prisoners whether the question was really what we expected from life. Was it not, rather, what life was expecting from us? I suggested that life was awaiting something from them. In fact, the woman was being awaited by her child abroad, and the man had a series of books he had begun to write and publish but had not yet finished.
>
> I have said that man should not ask what he may expect from life, but should rather understand that life expects something from him. It may also be put this way: in the last resort, man should not ask, 'What is the meaning of my life?' but should realize that he himself is being questioned. Life is putting its problems to him, and it is up to him to respond to these questions by being responsible; he can only answer to life by answering for *his* life.

Looked at in this way, life provides us with a wonderful purpose: to make the fullest use of it by serving others. I have been at the bedsides of many dying people, and it is obvious that some die in peace, and others in torment. The difference seems to lie in the way they spent their lives. Did they give their lives in service, or did they live selfishly?

To live selfishly is to be constantly aware of what we must give up, even if we do make sacrifices here and there. We end up seeing everything in terms of how it affects us. It is a way of life that yields precious little peace. Service to others saves us from this predicament, because it reminds us of what we are living for and helps us forget ourselves. It also gives us a new perspective – one that allows us to see the size of our life in relation to the rest of the universe.

True service is always an act of showing another person love. It is easy to forget this, even in a religious community like my own, where service is at the core of every member's daily life. Whenever we let our work become an end in itself, we lose sight of the love that gives it a deeper purpose and peace, and gradually it becomes a mindless, mechanical chore. With love, the most mundane task can take on meaning. Without it, the noblest task can become drudgery.

SOME TIME AGO I visited Plum Village, a Buddhist community in France. Each year hundreds of guests visit Plum Village. Some come for quiet meditation. Others join retreats led by Thich Nhat Hanh, the soft-spoken Vietnamese monk who heads the community (he is renowned for his leadership in the peace movement of the 1960s). Needless to say, the full-time residents – families and single people, as well as monks – are kept busy. Yet I was struck by the way they nurture an awareness of work as service.

There is always plenty to do at Plum Village, what with new buildings going up, renovations to be made on old houses, and several large orchards to maintain. Yet work for its own sake is frowned on. Rather than accepting the usual Western emphasis on what must be accomplished during the course of the day, the people of Plum Village cultivate the ideal of 'living in the present moment'. They try to see each situation, each action, each encounter with another human being as an opportunity to become 'more fully alive'. Karl Riedl, a resident, explained to me:

> The art of working in mindfulness helps us to reconsider the whole idea of being effective. It helps us question our obsession with goals and our idea that everything must be done 'just so'. It makes us look in a new light at the images we have of ourselves as good or not good at certain tasks, and helps uncover and recover the joy that should inspire everything we do – whether working in the greenhouse, chopping wood, cleaning toilets, writing or hanging out the wash. All too often, we do not work mindfully, and we let our busyness shatter our harmony and happiness.

A verse from the Plum Village chanting book sheds further light on this attitude and reveals the community's priorities, at least as far as service is concerned:

> I vow to offer joy to one person in the morning
> And to relieve the grief of one person in the afternoon.
> I vow to live simply and sanely,
> Content with few possessions.
> I vow to keep my body healthy.
> I vow to let go of all worries and anxieties
> In order to be light and free.

drained

14 Living on a Prayer

More things are wrought by prayer
Than this world dreams of.

ALFRED, LORD TENNYSON

There are times when, no matter what we try to do to bring it about, nothing seems to give us peace. Though we strive for simplicity and silence – for detachment from the worries around us or inside us – we still feel left with a void. At times like these, when every other recourse has failed, prayer may seem like our last resort. It is an admission of our inability to 'keep it together', and a petition for assistance from a stronger power.

I have known people who, when asked whether they pray, simply shrug off the question. 'What's the point?' they say. Yet others tell me that through prayer they gain a connection to God, and this fills their emptiness. For them, prayer is no last resort; it is a constant lifeline.

The Jewish philosopher Martin Buber says that whenever we pray, we should cry out, imagining ourselves as hanging from a cliff by our hair, with a tempest raging around us so violently that we are sure we have only a few seconds left to be saved.

Buber goes on, 'In truth there is no counsel, no refuge and no peace for anyone save to lift up his eyes and his heart to God and to cry out to him. One should do this at all times, for a man is in great danger in the world.'

Buber's image is dramatic, but it is not exaggerated. In a culture like ours, where the long arm of the mass media reaches so far that news of celebrity, scandal or catastrophe can stop millions of people in their tracks, the individual has never been so susceptible to the lure of following the crowd. Nietzsche saw this a hundred years ago when he mused on the truth of the old proverb, *Gemeinschaft macht gemein* – 'community makes common (crude)' and warned of the dangers of a society where mass-values are so strong that they can deaden even the strongest conscience or will.

It is all too easy to lose strength of character and succumb to what sociologists call the 'herd instinct': we fall prey to fear of others, to ambition, to the desire to please people. The constant traffic and opinions of those around us swamp our inner lives and finally drown them. We convince ourselves that we are our own masters, but in actual fact many of us cannot even think for ourselves. Our life consists merely (to quote Nietzsche again) of 'constant adjustments to all sorts of different collective influences and societal demands'.

But this need not be the case. These external influences and pressures can be warded off. Prayer is the best defence in the face of such onslaughts – as a protective armour around the quiet flame of the heart. And it is more: it is a life-giving and life-affirming discipline that can bring us to our senses – back to God – when we have gone astray. It focuses us and directs us to the source of peace. As Malcolm Muggeridge put it:

> In the turmoil of life without, and black despair within, it is always possible to turn aside and wait on God. Just as at the

centre of a hurricane there is stillness, and above the clouds a clear sky, so it is possible to make a little clearing in the jungle of our human will for a rendezvous with God. He will always turn up, though in what guise and in what circumstances cannot be foreseen – perhaps trailing clouds of glory, perhaps as a beggar; in the purity of the desert or in the squalor of London's Soho or New York's Times Square.

Prayer need not be formal. For my wife and me, it is the natural way we begin and end our day together; we pray every morning when we get up, and every evening before we go to bed. Some may pray more often than that, others less. Some people pray on their knees; others use a prayer book. Some speak; some do not actually use words at all. As long as our prayer is genuine, and not just an empty rite, it does not matter how we do it. The important thing is to make room for it, somewhere.

The Bible encourages people to 'pray without ceasing'. For some, this way of thinking is an obstacle. How does one pray all day? What does 'unceasingly' mean? For others, the idea is not only simple, but enlightening and refreshing. As James, a long-time friend, explains:

> Although I have prayed ever since I can remember, it was only when I began to understand prayer as a way of life – as a constant attitude rather than a repetitive action – that I understood the idea of praying without ceasing: it is an attitude to life.

In the same vein, someone told me recently, 'Prayer used to be when I would talk to God at certain times of the day – in the morning, or before I went to bed. Now I know that it is an all-day conversation. I pray as I walk through the airport or down the shopping-centre aisle.'

Nineteenth-century poet Gerard Manley Hopkins takes this idea further, suggesting that even the most menial tasks in our lives can be seen as a form of prayer. It all depends how we go about doing them:

> It is not only prayer that gives God glory, but work. Smiting on an anvil, sawing a beam, whitewashing a wall, driving horses, sweeping, scouring, everything gives God some glory if being in his grace you do it as your duty…. To lift up the hands in prayer gives God glory, but a man with a dung fork in his hand, a woman with a slop pail, give him glory too. He is so great that all things give him glory if you mean they should.

Each of us will pray differently. And as our circumstances change – through illness, old age or crisis, for instance – so may our prayers.

As a young American, Doug found little meaning in prayer. Upset by the hypocrisy he perceived in his mainstream church, he found himself increasingly at odds with most of the Christians he encountered in his youth, especially on the issue of military service. After the bombing of Pearl Harbor, his classmates and teachers at the University of North Carolina praised his refusal to be conscripted – they admired his determination to stand up for what he believed in, even if they personally disagreed with his deeply-held conviction that taking another human life was morally wrong. But his church saw things differently. They considered his actions to be nothing less than treason, motivated by plain old cowardice. The judge who tried and sentenced him as a felon for evading the draft was a member of his own congregation.

> There I sat in an antiquated county jail, in my home town of Lexington, Kentucky, with crab lice, awful food, a broken shower and no issue of clothes. Fortunately, my mother was able

to bring me soap and a change of underwear. It was the first, hardest period of my sentence, and was lightened only by listening day after day to the story of an utterly broken German immigrant on his way to an internment camp. A neighbour had falsely accused him of espionage.

Slowly, through my little bit of suffering – the endurance of tedium and filth, and our treatment not as men but as numbers – I was led to take an interest in this needy inmate in the next bed, and the joy that comes from living for others began to waken in me. I began to see what Thomas Kelly meant by living in the 'eternal now', for every inmate was constantly talking about the time left until his release, forever living in the future. When I began to live in the moment – not for release, not even for the next meal or movie or chance to sleep – it became possible for me to be at peace even in prison.

It was the first of many difficult periods of struggle in his life, and Doug slowly came to find hope and meaning in prayer.

It is not always a matter of words. Part of it is a quiet turning toward God throughout the day, an upward glance, a moment or two of silence remembering someone who is sick or suffering. Part of it might be considering various concerns and questions of the day. Part of it is asking for light to see my wrongs, to recognize where I might have hurt others. Prayer helps me strengthen my resolve to place others' needs above my own. And in all of this there is peace.

Swiss theologian Karl Barth once wrote that to clasp one's hands in prayer is the beginning of an uprising against the disorder of the world. If this is true, and I believe it is, then our prayer life cannot exist in a separate sphere from the rest of our lives, and our prayers must consist of more than longings or intentions. If we want them to have any real integrity or impact on the rest of the world, our prayers must develop into something more than just self-centred pleas for personal happiness. Prayer that doesn't spur us on to some kind of action is pure hypocrisy.

Doug hints at the importance of including others in our prayers. In the Jewish writings of the Old Testament and the Christian writings of the New, as well as down through the history of the persecuted Church and its many martyrs, we find the same thought, and an even more radical one: the practice of praying for our enemies, for those who persecute us and hurt us, whether through backbiting, slander, betrayal, physical violence or anything else.

Jim Wallis, a well-known writer and editor of *Sojourners* magazine in Washington, D.C., writes:

> As long as we do not pray for our enemies, we continue to see only our own point of view – our own righteousness – and to ignore their perspective. Prayer breaks down the distinctions between *us* and *them*. To do violence to others, you must make them enemies. Prayer, on the other hand, makes enemies into friends.

I remember an occasion during the Gulf War, right after the United States launched its full-scale ground attack on Iraq, in early 1991. Addressing the nation over network television, President Bush implored viewers to drop whatever they were doing and pray for 'our boys' in the Gulf. He ended his speech with a fervent 'God bless the United States of America'.

Most Americans probably stopped and fulfilled their patriotic duty without further thought. Yet as Thich Nhat Hanh has pointed out, there were probably equal numbers of Iraqi Muslims bowing to Allah just at that moment, sending up prayers

drained

on behalf of their husbands and sons. How would God decide which nation to support?

People pray to God because they want God to fulfil some of their needs. If they want to have a picnic, they may ask God for a clear, sunny day. At the same time, farmers who need more rain might pray for the opposite. If the weather is clear, the picnickers may say, 'God is on our side; he answered our prayers.' But if it rains, the farmers will say that God heard their prayers. This is the way we usually pray.

When you pray only for your own picnic and not for the farmers who need the rain, you are doing the opposite of what Jesus taught. Jesus said, 'Love your enemies, bless them that curse you.' When we look deeply into our anger, we see that the person we call our enemy is also suffering. As soon as we see that, we have the capacity of accepting and having compassion for him. Jesus called this 'loving your enemy'. When we are able to love our enemy, he or she is no longer our enemy. The idea of 'enemy' vanishes and is replaced by the notion of someone suffering a great deal who needs our compassion. Loving others is sometimes easier than we might think, but we need to practise it.

15 Lights, Camera

More and more I feel that the people of ill will
have used time much more effectively than have
the people of good will. We will have to repent in
this generation not merely for the hateful words
and actions of the bad people, but for the appalling
silence of the good people.

MARTIN LUTHER KING

I f anything is clear by this point, it should be that peace does
not mean inactivity. It is true that peace can include both
calm and repose. But does this restful peace suggest com-
placency, passivity?

The gift of peace is an answer to unfulfilled longing; it is an end
to the destructive wear-and-tear of doubt and wrongdoing. It
is wholeness and healing. But as much as it is all of these, peace
is also a call to action and new life. Peace may grow out of
meditation and prayer, but it cannot stop there. It brings new
obligations, new energy and new creativity. Like a seed beneath
the soil, it germinates silently and unseen, but then bursts with
vitality, unfurling, flowering and finally coming to fruit.

Once peace blossoms within us, it is up to us to see that we
share it. We who have received the gift of peace cannot keep it
to ourselves, shutting out the noise around us and ignoring the
plight of those who do not possess it.

Speaking from the perspective of engaged Buddhism, with its equal emphases on meditation and compassionate commitment to others, Thich Nhat Hanh recalls the Vietnam War and the dilemma it posed for him. Was the fruit of peace contemplation, or was it action?

> So many of our villages were being bombed. Along with my monastic brothers and sisters, I had to decide what to do. Should we continue to practise in our monasteries, or should we leave the meditation halls in order to help the people who were suffering under the bombs? After careful reflection, we decided to do both – to go out and help people, but to do so in a spirit of engaged mindfulness.... Once there is seeing, there must also be doing. Otherwise, what is the use of seeing?

If we seek to live in peace with our fellow human beings, certain inescapable responsibilities will fall on us, and we must grapple with them like Thich Nhat Hanh and his monks did. We cannot choose to live in harmony just with nature, or just with ourselves, to the exclusion of others.

When a person sets out to find peace, the search springs from the desire to find a deeper, more truly fulfilled life, not an emptier one. Ex-servicemen and business executives, housewives and ministers, high school dropouts and educated professionals have all told me the same: peace does not just mean saying no to violence, greed, sexual promiscuity or hypocrisy. It means saying yes to something that takes the place of all these.

In an earlier chapter I told the story of John Winter, a former lab employee who left his job after discovering that his firm was involved in munitions testing. He says:

> I rejected violence and began to look for peace, but soon I realized that peace is much more than the absence of war. I was tired of saying I couldn't join the army. What *could* I do? I

was seeking a practical alternative to war, not just an end to it. I wanted to commit myself to a different way. I wanted something to live for, not just something to fight against.

Without knowing what it is we are living for, we will almost certainly have a hard time putting up much of a fight against anything. Feelings of complete powerlessness and helplessness will cripple our ability to respond when challenging circumstances confront us: 'What can I do?' becomes our cry of despair.

In 1992, during the siege of Sarajevo, cellist Vedran Smailovic also voiced this cry, but not in hopeless resignation. Vedran formed his own unique response to the cruel, bloody reality surrounding him, acting out of deep conviction – doing exactly what he knew how to do.

Near my house in Sarajevo, there was a bread shop. On May 27, 1992, a long queue of people stood in front of that shop, waiting for a truck which would bring bread. They waited patiently and with dignity, though they waited long hours. But that was not the only tragedy. As though it were not enough to be hungry and miserable, instead of the bread, there came a terrible explosion. A shell, guided by the hand of a demon, exploded just steps away, killing twenty-two of those totally innocent, patient, hungry people.

In the first instant there was utter silence, shock. Then chaos –crying, screaming, yelling, shouting, blood – tangled bodies lying wounded, bleeding, dying, dead. In horror and panic some ran away. Some ran towards the massacre, trying to help the wounded. The first car arrived. Rescuers literally jumped over the dead bodies trying to put the wounded into the car, even into the boot. Another car came, then another. One of the rescuers was hit by sniper fire. First the seriously wounded, then those with minor injuries and finally the dead were taken away.

That night I couldn't sleep. Sitting, thinking about life, I couldn't understand why these innocent people, my good fellow citizens and next-door neighbours, with whom I had spent my childhood, should have their lives ended in such a terrible, terrible way. I understood only that in my town in time of war a life is worth absolutely nothing. Filled with sorrow I eventually fell asleep at dawn, and was awakened by new explosions and the shouts of my neighbours, who were carrying children and blankets to shelters. I went to the shelter myself and returned home after the shelling was over. I washed my face and hands, shaved, and without thinking, put on my white shirt, black evening suit and white bow tie, took my cello and left home.

Looking at the new ruins, I arrived at the place of the massacre. It was adorned with flowers, wreaths and peace messages; there were posters on local shops saying who had been killed. On a nearby table was a solemn book of condolences which people were signing. I opened my cello case and sat down, not knowing what I would play. Full of sadness and grief, I lifted my bow and spontaneously made music. I thought of the cruel fate of my neighbours, aware of the fact that the same or even worse could happen again at any moment. I was playing and crying at the same time, and the music, pouring from me like my tears, was Albinoni's 'Adagio'…the saddest, saddest music I know.

The passers-by stopped and listened and cried with me. They placed flowers, prayed, lit candles. When I finished playing there was no applause. I slowly rose, stood in silence for one minute and then put the instrument in its case. People gathered around me and we talked. Later, in a nearby café, friends asked me to play again, to repeat my music prayer for peace. They needed me to play – the music was healing them as well as me. I understood then that this was no longer a purely personal issue, and that was when I decided to play for twenty-two days in a row and to dedicate one day to each of my twenty-two fellow citizens killed in the bread-queue massacre.

So began Vedran's Music for Peace initiative, which would eventually earn him national and international recognition as the inspiration for civil resistance in Bosnia. Today he is celebrated around the world for his courageous act of protest; it has inspired poems and songs, stories and music. Still, Vedran insists he is 'ordinary, like any other', but he acknowledges that his upbringing in an exceptional family greatly helped prepare and empower him for non-violent social action.

His father, Avdo Smailovic, was an educator and former Yugoslavia's most acclaimed contemporary composer. His mother, Munira, he says, was 'not a musician, but a hero who raised musicians'. From childhood, Vedran and his sisters belonged to a family ensemble called 'Musica Ad Hominem' –Music for the People – formed by Avdo Smailovic to honour his heartfelt principle that good music and culture is not only the right of the rich and privileged, but belongs just as much to poor and uneducated people. The family troupe took their specially adapted cultural programmes to remote villages and farming communities, as well as to the most prestigious venues, performing as many as 180 concerts a year. So along with the music, Vedran inherited from his father a strong sensitivity toward injustice, as well as a deep feeling of humanitarian commitment. Often as a young adult he would sponsor and organize events to help people in need.

For Vedran, one of the greatest tragedies of Sarajevo's destruction was the shelling of the magnificent National and University Library, and he honoured the memory of his father in a very special way when he returned to mourn the ruin of that building, two days after it was gutted by fire.

The ruins of the National Library were still very hot and dangerous. But the atmosphere was extraordinary! Strong and powerful, sacred as a temple, at the same time so sad and glorious. It felt as if the outraged souls of all the authors of the burnt books were there in silent, warning witness to the world. I brought with me my cello and a portrait of my beloved father – painted by Dobrivoje Beljkasic, a renowned artist whose work, like all the art housed in the studios and galleries on the third floor, had been totally destroyed in the fire. The soul of my esteemed father was also there – in me, in my music and in Dobrivoje's paint-ing – and the spirit of all the painters, dead and alive. Nobody can destroy the soul, the spirit of art and creativity. My gesture symbolized that.

Later, when I finished playing, I brought my father's portrait home. Then I returned to the place of the massacre and paused just for a moment, before once more playing Albinoni.

Vedran kept up his Music for Peace efforts until December 1993, when it finally became possible for him to leave Sarajevo. From then on, even though he was without a cello at first, he has persisted in bringing music to people around the world, moving between the biggest concert halls and the poorest plac-es. He still carries the inspiration of his father and Musica Ad Hominem deep in his soul.

Vedran now lives in Northern Ireland, where he has found time to record several albums. (His 'Sarajevo/Belfast' is a joint venture with folk-singer Tommy Sands.) Crossing barriers of culture and language, his music continues to defy and inspire, to mourn and sing.

> I worry about the human race and the damage we will continue to do in the name of progress. I worry. And I am afraid. But I offer my music. That is still what I know best how to do.

Author Amy Carmichael uses the imagery of a battlefield to de-scribe peace. She says that it's not the soldier lying in bed while the battle is on who has peace, but those who give their lives on the field. Those who fight closest to the captain are most likely to be wounded, but they will also have the greatest peace.

Jonathan Kuttab, a Palestinian lawyer, affirms the truth of this statement from his own experience. I have met him several times during my trips to the Middle East, and each encounter has deepened my respect for him. His courage on behalf of his people, who suffer discrimination and abuse at the hands of the Israeli government – and his unwillingness to back down, even when the odds are stacked high against him – place him on the frontline of the struggle for justice in his homeland. Following Jesus' example, Jonathan firmly believes in the power of non-violence: it is a force, he says, that is stronger than the bulldozers that come to clear space for settlers, destroying the homes and lives of countless Palestinians.

When clients come to me for help in trying to protect their homes, I have to tell them that the law isn't going to be very helpful, since it wasn't written to defend their rights. What is helpful, I tell them, is to stand non-violently, and even to lie down in front of the bulldozers, if need be.

I gave this advice to some people from one particular village, and not long afterward I got a call saying, 'The settlers and soldiers and bulldozers are here, and we are trying to stop them.' So I got into my car and drove over as fast as I could and met the man who had telephoned me.

When we arrived at the site, there was nobody around. (I didn't know that the soldiers had arrived earlier and had arrested all the protestors.) There was only a man in a bulldozer, beginning to tear up the ground, and an armed settler guarding the area. So I marched right up and said, 'You can't do this, you have no right. This is my land.' (Of course, the land actually belonged to my client.) And he says, 'Get out of here. We're working!' So I went and stood right in front of the bulldozer, and I got the man who was with me to stand at the back. Well, the driver didn't want any trouble, so he got out. Then the settler came over and climbed into the cab. He revved up the engine. I looked around. There was nobody. We were out in the wilderness – no CNN, no newspaper reporters, absolutely *nobody* around. I took a deep breath and said to myself, 'This is a good day to die.' I really thought I was going to get killed.

I told the other man to run to the village and see if he could get some other people to come out. So there I was, left alone with the bulldozer and the angry settler. But I did feel peace. I was so calm, so peaceful.

With no one behind him now, the settler backed up the bulldozer and tried to go around. But I moved in front of him again and stood there. And then a great idea came to me: I just turned my back on him, because something told me that it's very hard to kill a man who's not even looking at you. I turned my back and folded my hands and refused to move.

There was a pile of rubble that the settler was trying to shift, and I was defending that pile of rubble. It was a strange feeling, very peaceful, very wonderful. The settler would rev up the engine and just come straight at me, but then he would stop.

Non-violence is powerful. The media and publicity help strengthen it, but it has power in and of itself. The settler in that bulldozer wanted me to pick up a stone, he wanted me to yell and curse him. Had I done so, he would have killed me in a second, I am sure. But I stayed calm, just stood there quietly. 'I am not going to let you move that rubble.'

After about half an hour the man who had gone to the village returned with the military governor and a number of other people in jeeps. So I said, 'Look, I am a lawyer. This is my client's land, and I don't allow you to come in.' They said, 'Well, there are courts…' And I said, 'Fine, go to court. This is my land.' I refused to budge, and eventually the military governor talked the settler into taking the bulldozer away.

THERE IS A FALSE PEACE, supported by the rich and powerful, by the oppressors, the status quo. For them, peace is maintaining power, maintaining their oppression, so that nothing creates waves or disturbs their control. Any attempt to challenge their authority is portrayed as a breach of peace. But true peace isn't about 'maintaining' or 'keeping' peace; it's about making peace. Sometimes you have to be assertive; there's nothing passive about working for peace. You have to have a firm internal stability – an internal peace of mind – and an assurance that you are doing the right thing. This allows you to be at ease, even in the most confrontational situations. Without this, you very easily fall into the trap of becoming as bad as the evil you're trying to oppose.

If you allow anger, bitterness, hatred, selfishness or self-centredness to set in, then it's very easy to cross the line. You will be using the same tools and methods as your oppressors, and your actions will be no better. I feel that the minute I succumb to hatred and bitterness, I have lost and they have won. I have lost – no matter what skirmishes or battles I win – because they have shown that their way is right, that I have to be more violent and more aggressive than they are.

I can't claim to have placed my life directly on the line too many times. But that day in front of the bulldozer – for me it was a strange experience. I felt a deep sense of inner peace. I literally took a deep breath, looked up at the nice blue sky, and said, 'It's a good day to die.' And, like never before in my life, I felt the real power of peace.

People talk about peace all the time; everybody wants it, no one is against it. But how many of us are ready, like Jonathan, to put our lives on the line for it? For each person, the call to action will take a unique form. For one it may lead to activism; for the next, to community; for the next, to an entirely different calling. It may simply mean being a voice of reconciliation at one's place of work, or trying to be more forgiving and loving at home.

A great deed may be nobler than an ordinary, unnoticed one, but it can distract us from the things we ought to be doing right around us. It can even produce a hardness of heart toward those who need us most. French writer Jean Vanier warns:

> Sometimes it is easier to hear the cries of the poor and oppressed who are far away than the cries of people in our own community. There is nothing very splendid in responding to the person who is with us day after day and who gets on our nerves.

No matter where we are or what we do, true peace will only come about if we are prepared to work and make sacrifices. For unlike false peace that commits to nothing and jumbles everything into confusion, true peace comes like a bracing wind that sets into motion everything in its path.

drained

16 Say You Want a Revolution

One has to have a great dose of humanity, a great
dose of the feeling of justice and of truth not to fall
into extreme dogmatism, into a cold scholasticism, into
isolation from the masses. Every day one has to struggle in order for this love of humanity to be transformed
into concrete deeds, into acts that serve as examples,
as a moving force.

CHE GUEVARA

O f all the slogans I have heard at demonstrations
and rallies held by peace activists over the last
few decades, one of the simplest and strongest
is 'No Justice, No Peace'. If it is important to talk
or write about peace, then working for it in some practical way
is even more important. But when all is said and done, peace is
real only insofar as it gives birth to justice.

In the same way as the injustices of social inequality, oppression, slavery and war go hand in hand with strife and division,
so peace must go hand in hand with justice, because justice
flourishes where these things are overcome.

To many people, peace means national security, stability,
law and order. It is associated with education, culture and civic
duty, prosperity and health, comfort and quiet. It is the good
life. But can a peace based on these things be shared by all? If
the good life means limitless choices and excessive consump-
tion for a privileged few, it follows that it must mean hard labour

and grinding poverty for millions of others. Can this be peace? Or justice?

Writing in Germany on the eve of World War II, my grandfather stated:

> If I really want peace, I must represent it in all areas of life. I cannot represent a pacifism that maintains there will be no more war. This claim is not valid; there is war right up to the present day. I have no faith in the pacifism of businessmen who beat down their competitors, or husbands who cannot even live in peace and love with their own wives.
>
> When over a thousand people have been killed unjustly, without trial, under Hitler's new government, isn't that already war?
>
> When hundreds of thousands of people in concentration camps are robbed of their freedom and stripped of all human dignity, isn't that war?
>
> When in Asia millions of people starve to death while in North America and elsewhere millions of tons of wheat are stockpiled, isn't that war?
>
> When thousands of women prostitute their bodies and ruin their lives for the sake of money; when millions of babies are aborted each year, isn't that war?
>
> When people are forced to work like slaves because they can hardly provide the milk and bread for their children, isn't that war?
>
> When the wealthy live in villas surrounded by parks, while in other districts some families have only one room to share, isn't that war?
>
> When one person builds up a huge bank account while another earns scarcely enough for basic necessities, isn't that war?
>
> When reckless drivers cause thousands of traffic deaths every year, isn't that war?

Given the state of our planet today, it is not surprising that people dismiss both peace and justice as utopian foolishness. How can anyone be at peace, they ask, when turmoil and anguish are everywhere, and weapons of mass destruction – held by an increasing number of countries – mock the very idea of human survival? How can there be justice, when the whims of a shrinking handful of wealthy and powerful individuals wreak havoc with the lives of millions around the globe?

Unless peace is accompanied by justice, it is no more than an empty phrase. As the Jewish prophet Jeremiah complained, "'Peace, peace,' they say; yet there is no peace.' If we are sincere about wanting peace, not only for ourselves but for others as well, then we will recognize that a new relationship among people is necessary.

Tom Kelly and James Tate are living examples of the transformation that can come about when the true meaning of peace strikes a person's heart. Born in Belfast, Northern Ireland, each grew up wanting peace and security for their country. But though they lived within minutes of each other, they grew up in different worlds. Tom's family is Catholic, James's is Protestant. Yet except for some names, their stories are startlingly alike. Tom begins:

> In 1969, around the time the Troubles broke out, I was just leaving school. IRA slogans started appearing on walls. I couldn't understand what it was all about. My father and mother hadn't taught us children bigotry. When I asked my dad, he pleaded with me not to get involved; it wasn't of God, he said.
>
> As the Troubles went on, I noticed the mounting hysteria in my neighbourhood of Belfast, Turf Lodge. There were men

running in the streets with rifles and handguns, and they'd set landmines behind barricades. A lot of images of confrontations between Nationalists and Loyalists were flashed on the TV, and later, after the British Army and the RUC (Royal Ulster Constabulary) moved in, things got even more tense. The media projected a sense of confusion, and for the first time I sensed a threat, even though I didn't know what I was panicking about.

I was fifteen years old. I knew some of my friends had joined the junior ranks of the IRA, and I decided to join with them. I learned to break down weapons and was soon inducted into the ranks of the Provisional IRA. I fired my first shot and was introduced to violence. I knew right then that my life was on the line, because many bullets flew past me when I was firing.

They taught me that we were fighting for a socialist republic. I didn't know anything about socialism, communism or any other *ism*. To me, that stuff was for the smart guys. I just perceived myself as a soldier, defending my own area.

James grew up with an intense loathing of Catholics, without ever having met one. 'I inherited a lot of bigotry from my mum,' he says. 'She had been brought up in the Loyalist tradition and had been taught to distrust Catholics, as had everyone else who lived in my area.'

I was raised in Sandy Row, a working-class area of Belfast. Everyone called themselves Protestants, but very few ever went to church. Our family certainly didn't. It's a strange thing: I grew up hating Catholics, but I'd never met one. It was a blind hatred. There were no Catholics at my school or youth club; we didn't mix.

In my early teens, I did what was expected of me and joined the Orange Order, participating in the marches with the band, everyone decked out in coloured hats and whatnot. And then

1969 came along, and the struggle for civil rights. It quickly escalated into riots and clashes with the British Army and the police. In response to the IRA's bombing campaign, groups of Loyalist men, like myself, started forming paramilitary organizations. I ended up joining the UVF (Ulster Volunteer Force). The idea was pretty simple: if the IRA bombed somewhere in the Protestant community, we would bomb somewhere in a Catholic area. And that's how it developed. Eventually I was arrested in my home on weapons charges. It was on an Easter Sunday morning. The British Army searched my house, and they found five guns.

As a result of their paramilitary involvement, both Tom and James wound up behind barbed wire, in internment camps, prisoners of a British Army that viewed them as common criminals. Tom was set free after two and a half years. During his imprisonment, his resentment and hatred toward the British Army and the Loyalist paramilitaries had only intensified. Once out, he went straight back into the IRA, became more heavily involved than before – and ended up looking at ten years in jail.

James, on the other hand, was released after five years of imprisonment, and he decided he'd had enough. He headed home to his wife, broke ties with the UVF and tried to establish himself in 'normal' life. Though his prison record made the task difficult, he eventually found work through a church-sponsored jobs programme. Then, one day, a change occurred:

> I was sitting in the transport van with an older man, one of the managers, and he started to tell me his life story. It was a tremendous story: he'd been involved with drug trafficking in Afghanistan and had been set upon, robbed and left to die.

Some people had rescued him and brought him home to Ireland. And through this experience, he'd become a practising Christian. He was telling me this, and then I realized out of the blue that this man was a Catholic. The people who had rescued him had been Catholics. Before I realized it I was sitting there in that van crying. And then I just started to tell him all my past, where I'd been and what I'd done and everything else. Tears rolled down my face, and I didn't know why.

Bit by bit, events took place that chiselled away James's bigotry and hate. He came to recognize his own need for forgiveness and a new start. God touched his heart, he says, and this made him look at other people in a new light.

Tom's life, meanwhile, had undergone an equally radical change of course. His years 'inside' showed him just how meaningless and senseless violence is – no matter whose side instigates it. And he had also made a conscious decision to let God guide his life. So when Tom met James at an interdenominational meeting, they embraced like long-lost brothers. Strange behaviour for two men who were once determined to kill each other…

Today, they spend a lot of time together; after all, their homes never were far apart. Often they are invited to speak at gatherings, and many have been encouraged by hearing their life stories. For Tom and James, the fight for their homeland is no longer about allegiances and boundaries. It's got more to do with bringing hearts together and finding common ground. To use James's words:

We in Northern Ireland need to start again from the beginning. There's more that holds us together than holds us apart. We need to put our two communities together, because ignorance is what

drained

builds mistrust. Let the children grow up together, and they'll soon see there's no difference between them.

SOME TIME AGO I travelled to Mexico's southernmost state of Chiapas to meet with Bishop Samuel Ruiz García. Don Samuel, as he is known, has been nominated for the Nobel Peace Prize on account of his work with the people there, especially the indigenous peasants who populate the region's impoverished mountain villages.

Don Samuel is dedicated, very simply, to what he calls the twofold task of peace and justice. That task has included acting as a mediator between Mexican society and the Zapatistas, a grassroots movement organized to fight for some of the basic human rights most of us take for granted, such as land ownership and access to medical care. Not surprisingly, his outspokenness has earned him hatred and harassment, especially from the repressive local government, and he has been the target of at least two assassination attempts in recent years. In a conversation we had in December 1997, Don Samuel told me:

Peace for humanity is not only the absence of war, or the end of violence. The Romans said, 'If you want peace, prepare to fight.' For them peacetime was the time to prepare for war. It is for us, too, but in a different way. For us peace demands a new social order.

It demands a new, brotherly relationship among people. And it requires a change in the oppressive socio-economic structure.

The poor define the history of human society. A man is poor as a result of a social conflict. There is a system that makes him poor, a system that deprives him. If in a society the poorest person is the reference point for the common good, then we have a society that is doing its task. But if in a society the poor man is squashed on the floor, that society is opposed to peace.

It is this inexcusable suffering (in whatever form it takes) and the selfishness that causes it that propels people like Don Samuel to stand up and speak out. They know that a real, lasting 'peace' must do something to address the imbalances of our society. Often, such people are met with deaf ears. Prejudice and fear lead people to shut out their message, to dismiss them. Some even go so far as to silence them by killing them. Don Samuel knows that his time may soon run out. Yet he carries on. 'Peace,' he says, 'is a task; it is work that we have to develop. It is not a question of doctrine, but of practice.'

Palestinian activist Elias Chacour offers further insight:

drained

Peace is linked to so many problems, risks and hard work. The Aramaic word *ashrei* doesn't only mean 'happy'; it has a relationship with *yashar,* from the Hebrew 'straight': straightening yourself up. Therefore, if you are hungry and thirsty for justice, you must straighten yourself up and act to provide yourself and your people with that justice. The same is true of peace. It is not said, 'Happy are the peace-contemplators,' but, 'Happy are the peacemakers.' In other words, get up and do something.

Epilogue: Keep the Faith

Hope is the thing left to us in a bad time.

IRISH PROVERB

On the last day of 1997, hundreds of Tzotzil Indians walked in a memorial procession to the village of Acteal, in Chiapas, Mexico, where forty-five of their compatriots – mostly women and children – had been brutally killed by a local pro-government militia just nine days before. Living in an isolated area where political repression has resulted in one 'disappearance' after another, the participants knew they were not marching without danger.

Unarmed, the marchers were doubly vulnerable because of their position: though supportive of the goals of local Zapatista freedom-fighters, they remained opposed to violence and were thus accused by both sides of partisanship and disloyalty. Yet the procession was not just a gamble. It was an act of defiance undertaken in a spirit of determination and hope.

A sign on a wooden cross at the head of the crowd read, 'It is time to harvest, time to build,' and many of the men carried bricks ('to symbolize the weight of our suffering,' one said) which they planned to use to build a shrine for the dead. Several planned to resettle in the village, though they knew they might have to flee again. And carrying a cracked statue of the Virgin Mary 'in the name of peace', they remained committed to non-violence.

Who were these courageous men and women who could stare death so calmly in the face? Was their peace the mark of some strange martyr-like strength? Was it a sign of insanity? Maybe they simply felt like American peace activist Liz Mc-Alister, who wrote the following after her husband's recent imprisonment for his participation in an anti-military demonstration:

> God's vision – more, God's promise – of a humane and just society is a promise on which we can bet our lives. None of us can be content until this promise is a reality for all people and for all our earth. So you stake your life on the vision of God in Isaiah, the days to come when people will beat swords into ploughshares and spears into pruning hooks; so we endure and are carried by our God in that endurance. Putting flesh on God's vision today, you are part of bringing it into being – no more, no less.

Peace is a relentless pursuit kept up only by hope and courage, vision and commitment. But it is also a life-giving power. It heals what is broken, replenishes what is used up and unleashes what is knotted and bound. Peace brings hope where there is despair, harmony where there is discord, love where there is hatred. It brings wholeness where there is fragmentation, consistency where there is compromise and deceit. Peace penetrates every sphere of existence, the spiritual as well as the material, the material as well as the spiritual. If it does not accomplish this transformation, it is not true peace at all, but sheer fancy.

Francis of Assisi held a keen awareness of what true peace demands. Though today he is best known as a harmless friar, a kind of medieval Dr. Doolittle who talked with animals and birds, St. Francis was no mild-mannered poet but a passionate soul. His search for peace led him to identify with the poor by giving up not only his inheritance, but even the very clothes off his back. His last will and testament was so unsparing in its condemnation of wealth and institutional religion that it was confiscated and burnt before he was deemed 'safe' for sainthood. And the words of the famous prayer attributed to him reveal a depth of spirit that still extends a challenge to us every time we read them – never mind how trite they have been made by overuse.

> Lord, make me an instrument of thy peace!
> Where there is hatred, let me sow love;
> Where there is injury, pardon;
> Where there is doubt, faith;
> Where there is despair, hope;
> Where there is darkness, light;
> And where there is sadness, joy.
> O divine Master –
> Grant that I may not so much seek
> To be consoled, as to console;
> To be understood, as to understand;
> To be loved, as to love.
> For it is in giving that we receive,
> In pardoning that we are pardoned,
> And in dying that we are born to eternal life.

Peace is cosmic in aim, but it begins quietly, sometimes imperceptibly, from within. It transforms people and structures. Where peace rules, there is unity of self with true self, man with woman, humanity with creation and God.

None of this can happen by itself, or in a vacuum. Throughout this book we have seen that the way of peace has little or nothing to do with passivity or resignation. Peace is not for the spineless or self-absorbed, or for those content with a quiet life. True peace demands that we live honestly – before others and in the light of our own conscience. Thus the search for it cannot be a selfish one. It cannot be merely a question of achieving closure, finding fulfilment or, as Aristotle put it, 'actualizing our human potential'. No! To seek peace means to seek harmony within ourselves, with others and ultimately with God.

Grandiose as this sounds, it is really very simple. If we do not have peace, it is probably because we have forgotten to love one another. And there is really no excuse for that. I do not believe that anyone is so lacking in ability that they cannot love.

But perhaps the most important lesson I have learnt from the people whose stories I've told in this book consists in this: never give up; never lose heart, no matter what happens. It is this attitude that has carried countless individuals through the toughest of times. It can do the same for us too.

Rabbi Hugo Gryn, a survivor of the Holocaust, learnt the importance of hope as a young boy in Auschwitz, where he was imprisoned in the same barracks as his father:

> Despite the unspeakable conditions, many Jews, including my father, held on to whatever observances they could. One midwinter evening an inmate reminded him that it was soon the first night of Chanukah, the feast of lights. Over the next days my father constructed a small menorah of metal scraps. For a wick, he took threads from his prison uniform. Instead of oil, he somehow managed to wheedle butter from a guard.
>
> Such observances were strictly *verboten,* but we were used to taking risks. What I protested was the 'waste' of precious

calories. Would it not be better to share the butter on a crust of bread than to burn it?

'Hugo,' said my father, 'both you and I know that a person can live a very long time without food. But I tell you, a person cannot live a single day without hope. This oil will kindle a flame of hope. Never let hope die out. Not here; not anywhere. Remember this.'

Rabbi Gryn's story touches on a truth discovered by many before and after him: ultimately, it is hope that makes it possible for us to live from day to day; it is hope that urges us on, across life's stepping stones. It is hope that gives us the strength and ability to love, acting as the gateway to peace.

In a passage in *The Brothers Karamazov*, Fyodor Dostoevsky writes with similar hope and conviction. The conversation is between Father Zossima and a mysterious stranger, who speaks first:

'Until you have become really, in actual fact, a brother to everyone, brotherhood will not come to pass. No sort of scientific teaching, no kind of common interest, will ever teach people to share property and privileges with equal consideration for all. Everyone will think his share too small, and they will always be envying, complaining, and attacking one another. You ask when it will come to pass. It will come to pass, but first we have to go through the period of isolation.'

'What do you mean by isolation?' I asked him.

'Why, the isolation that prevails everywhere, above all in our age – it has not fully developed, it has not reached its limit yet. For everyone strives to keep his individuality as apart as possible. Everyone wishes to secure the greatest possible fullness of life for himself and forgets that true security is to be found in social solidarity rather than in isolated individual efforts. But this terrible individualism must inevitably have an end, and suddenly all will understand how unnaturally they are separated from one another. It will be the spirit of the time, and people will marvel that they have sat so long in darkness without seeing the light....

'But until then, we must keep the banner flying. Sometimes, even if he has to do it alone, and his conduct seems to be crazy, a man must set an example, and so draw people's souls out of their solitude, and spur them to some act of brotherly love, that the great idea may not die.'

drained

The Author

Life has taught me that active loving
saves one from a morbid preoccupation
with the shortcomings of society.

ALAN PATON

A NATURAL STORYTELLER, Johann Christoph Arnold infuses his writing with anecdotes gleaned from his years of community living and his experience as a counsellor. His books cut to the heart of real-life issues – sex, family, dying – and offer hope-filled alternatives in a desperate age.

Known for his unflinching stand on the side of oppressed people worldwide and his consistent respect for all life, he has appeared on numerous TV and radio broadcasts across the United States, Australia, Britain, Ireland and continental Europe.

Arnold lives at the Woodcrest Bruder-hof in New York, one of eight communities that form an international movement committed to a life of non-violence and simplicity, based on Jesus' teachings. Ever since the first Bruderhof ('place of brothers') was founded in Germany, in 1920, community members have rejected private property, opting instead to pool not only their money and possessions, but their time and talents as well. At the heart of their commitment is a deep-seated dedication to service, family and love of neighbour.

135

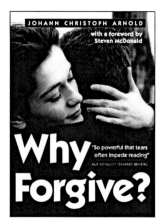

Why Forgive?

Johann Christoph Arnold

Foreword by Steven McDonald

IN **WHY FORGIVE? ARNOLD AVOIDS** glib pronouncements by letting the untidy experiences of ordinary people speak for themselves – people who have earned the right to talk about overcoming hurt, and about the peace of mind they have found in doing so. "Hurt" is an understatement, actually, for these stories deal with the harrowing effects of violent crime, betrayal, abuse, bigotry, gang warfare, and genocide.

But *Why Forgive?* examines life's more mundane battle scars as well: the wounds caused by backbiting, gossip, strained family ties, marriages gone cold and tensions in the workplace. As in life, not every story has a happy ending – a fact Arnold refuses to skirt. The book also addresses the difficulty of forgiving oneself, the futility of blaming God, and the turmoil of those who simply cannot forgive, even though they try.

Why Forgive? Read these stories, and decide for yourself.

Escape Routes

For People Who Feel Trapped in Life's Hells

Johann Christoph Arnold

EVERY ONE OF US HAS EXPERIENCED longer or shorter periods of anxiety, anger, guilt, discouragement, or loneliness. In forty years as a pastor, Johann Christoph Arnold has seen it all. But he's also witnessed the most hopeless lives completely transformed. That's why he is convinced that, no matter what problems you currently face, you too can find the freedom, confidence, and fulfillment that you long for.

In *Escape Routes*, Arnold tells real-life stories of people who have found their way out of life's hells despite the odds. This isn't a self-help book. It offers no quick fixes or superficial makeovers. But if you're ready to take its medicine, it will guide you on your way to a more hopeful and meaningful life.

Arnold writes: "Call it life, call it hell: there's not a person I've met who hasn't been lonely, discouraged, depressed, or guilt-ridden at one time or another, if not sick, burned-out, or at sea in a relationship. Sometimes I know this because they have told me about their problems; sometimes I can tell just by looking in their eyes. That's what got me started on this book – the fact that all of us have known some form of hell in our lives, and that insofar as any of us find freedom, confidence, companionship, and community, we will also know happiness."

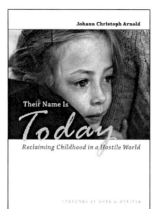

Their Name Is Today

Reclaiming Childhood in a Hostile World

Johann Christoph Arnold

Foreword by Mark K. Shriver

THERE'S HOPE FOR CHILDHOOD. Despite a perfect storm of hostile forces that are robbing children of a healthy childhood, courageous parents and teachers who know what's best for children are turning the tide.

Johann Christoph Arnold, whose books on education, parenting, and relationships have helped more than a million readers through life's challenges, draws on the stories and voices of parents and educators on the ground, and a wealth of personal experience. He surveys the drastic changes in the lives of children, but also the groundswell of grassroots advocacy and action that he believes will lead to the triumph of common sense and time-tested wisdom.

Their Name Is Today takes on technology, standardized testing, overstimulation, academic pressure, marketing to children, over-diagnosis and much more, calling on everyone who loves children to combat these threats to childhood and find creative ways to help children flourish. Every parent, teacher, and childcare provider has the power to make a difference, by giving children time to play, access to nature, and personal attention, and most of all, by defending their right to remain children.

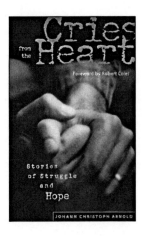

Cries from the Heart

Stories of Struggle and Hope

Johann Christoph Arnold

Foreword by Robert Coles

CRIES FROM THE HEART ANSWERS A SPECIFIC HUNGER millions share - a longing for a personal connection to the divine. In times of crisis, all of us reach for someone, or something, greater than ourselves. Some call it prayer. Others just do it. For many, it's often like talking to a wall. People are looking for assurance that someone hears them when they cry out in their despair, loneliness, or frustration. The last thing they need is another book telling them how to pray or what to say, holding out religion like a good-luck charm.

Instead of theorizing or preaching, Johann Christoph Arnold tells stories about real men and real women dealing with adversity. Their difficulties - which range from extreme to quite ordinary and universal - resonate with readers, offering a challenge, but also comfort and encouragement. People will see themselves in these glimpses of anguish, triumph, and peace.

Find more at www.plough.com

Lightning Source UK Ltd.
Milton Keynes UK
UKOW03f1550300517

302322UK00002B/8/P